FREELY
DETERMINED

FREELY DETERMINED

WHAT THE NEW PSYCHOLOGY OF THE SELF TEACHES US ABOUT HOW TO LIVE

KENNON M. SHELDON

BASIC BOOKS

New York

Basic Books
Hachette Book Group
1290 Avenue of the Americas, New York, NY 10104
www.basicbooks.com
Printed in the United States of America

First Edition: October 2022

Published by Basic Books, an imprint of Perseus Books, LLC, a subsidiary of Hachette Book Group, Inc. The Basic Books name and logo is a trademark of the Hachette Book Group.

The Hachette Speakers Bureau provides a wide range of authors for speaking events. To find out more, go to www.hachettespeakersbureau.com or call (866) 376-6591.

The publisher is not responsible for websites (or their content) that are not owned by the publisher.

Library of Congress Cataloging-in-Publication Data

Names: Sheldon, Kennon M. (Kennon Marshall), author.
Title: Freely determined : what the new psychology of the self teaches us about how to live / Kennon M. Sheldon.
Description: First edition. | New York : Basic Books, 2022. | Includes bibliographical references and index.
Identifiers: LCCN 2022006150 | ISBN 9781541620360 (hardcover) | ISBN 9781541620377 (ebook)
Subjects: LCSH: Free will and determinism. | Psychology.
Classification: LCC BF620 .S44 2022 | DDC 123/.5—dc23/eng/20220624
LC record available at https://lccn.loc.gov/2022006150

ISBNs: 9781541620360 (hardcover), 9781541620377 (ebook)

LSC-C

Printing 1, 2022

*To my father, John Donaldson, who started me
on this curious path.*

Man's main task in life is to give birth to himself, to become what he potentially is. The most important product of his effort is his own personality.

—Erich Fromm, *Man for Himself* (1947)

CONTENTS

INTRODUCTION

WHY FREE WILL MATTERS

When I was a teenager, my father and I used to argue about the existence of free will. My father, a staunch determinist, was convinced it was a myth. Our behavior might be caused by many factors, he said—genetics, environment, past conditioning—but human striving is not one of them. Not only do our choices not matter, they aren't even choices at all.

Our conversations took a similar path each time the subject arose. My father would repeat two simple questions. First he would ask, "Are there any uncaused causes?" In other words, are there any events that were not themselves caused by prior events? The answer had to be no. I picked up the coffee cup because of an unconscious habit, or because of my addiction to caffeine. My sense that *I* was the one choosing was merely a side effect of those prior causes, just as smoke is only a side effect of fire.

For his second question, my father would ask, "Does the present always follow the past?" I would have to agree that it did. "Then," he would conclude, "how could a person's feeling of causing their own behavior in the present be correct?" The present can only be what the past allows it to be, not what we want it to be.

My dad's arguments had definite intellectual appeal. They seemed to derive from logic, and from a scientific worldview that I strongly valued and believed in. In science, when objective facts contradict your subjective beliefs, then you need to change your beliefs. No wishful thinking allowed—better to be wrong than ignorant.

Still, my whole life, I have been haunted and hounded by the question of free will. Does an objective attitude *really* require us to deny all power to subjective intentions, to the sense that we are making choices in the world? Or can it be scientifically legitimate to conclude that a carefully thought out personal decision made a large difference in a person's life? These tensions have inspired a great deal of my research as a psychologist—they helped steer me toward the field of psychology in the first place.

Like me, you may also have trouble accepting determinism, at least the "hard" versions, which say that human consciousness is only a hallucination, and our ability to choose our own destiny a delusion. You feel more or less in charge of your life. Every day, you make decisions, from which shirt to wear in the morning to whether to pursue a particular job or relationship. You recognize that there are constraints on your choices, of course—you wouldn't wear a heavy coat on an eighty-degree day, or a pair of swim trunks to the office. And you know that just because you choose to go after something doesn't mean you'll get it. You may even realize, immediately or later on, that you made a wrong choice. Still, you are the one deciding, for better or worse. It might feel so obvious that you're tempted to see the whole free-will debate as pointless and irrelevant. What difference does it even make?

But if we dig a little deeper, free will gets more interesting— and we begin to see how crucial it is to who we are. If the determinist perspective is correct, for example, then our belief that we are making our own choices *must* be delusional. You might think that you started reading this book because that's what you decided to do today. But perhaps another factor, or combination of factors, is really at work: the firing of specific neurons, the release of certain neurochemicals, your past conditioning, your needy emotional state, your current course assignment, or the repeated insistence of a friend. In that case, the feeling that you caused yourself to start reading this book may simply be a comforting fairy tale, a mistaken attribution that allows you to maintain a sense that you are in control, but that ultimately holds you back. This is what hard determinists insist. Most of them put our belief in free will (including *yours*, dear reader!) into the same category as belief in telepathy and clairvoyance, in crystal healing or reincarnation, or in ghosts, spirits, and gods. They think you'd be better off if you could get over it.

As a research psychologist, I am just as skeptical as any other scientist about clairvoyance, reincarnation, deities, and the like. But my research has led me to suspect that the deterministic view of self-determination (namely, that there is no such thing) might just be wrong. Not only might we have free will, we might have *radical*, even *inescapable* free will—meaning that we can't help but make choices, on a daily and even moment-to-moment basis. That is what our minds evolved to do. And these choices can have a profound effect on the course of our lives—even when, at first glance, they appear very simple or minor.

Meet Tony, a college basketball player at a well-regarded state university. Tony is the best player on his team, and he hopes to be able to play professionally after graduation—he imagines himself in the NBA, with all the money and attention that would entail. Tony's teammates know he has this ambition, as does his coach. Unfortunately, Tony's team has played below expectations this season, and is in danger of being left out of the upcoming national championship tournament.

In a critical conference game, late in the season, Tony is dribbling the ball up the court. His team is behind by a point, and with only fifteen seconds left, this is their last chance to win (or at least tie) the game. Tony dribbles around the perimeter, looking for an opening in which to drive, or a teammate to pass to. With three seconds left, Alain, the team's small forward, cuts toward the basket, a step ahead of his defender. The opponent who is guarding Tony moves toward Alain, giving Tony the opportunity to take a challenging thirty-foot shot. Tony is a good shooter, but Alain is much closer to the basket. What will he do—shoot, or pass?

In one sense, this decision seems like it is Tony's alone. He's the one holding the ball at the critical moment. But in another sense, Tony's decision might not be his at all. It could be the product of countless possible factors independent of his consciousness. Maybe his body is exhausted, causing him to take the easier path of passing. Maybe his coach has told him to be bold in such situations, so he takes the shot. Maybe Tony is close friends with Alain; they've practiced this pass forever, and passing the ball to him is almost reflex. Or Tony could be a narcissist who craves attention and glory, so instead he takes the shot himself. Or perhaps the crowd is screaming so loudly that Tony gets distracted, and mishandles the ball before he even has a chance to shoot or pass. Tony's "decision," whatever it is, might really be anything *but* his decision. Just as you might not have caused yourself to pick up this book a few minutes ago, perhaps Tony didn't cause his own behavior: he was just a puppet, being controlled by factors outside his conscious awareness.

But let's say Tony takes the long shot. If he makes the shot, his team wins the game; if he misses, they lose. In the scenario where Tony makes the shot, he is a hero! The home crowd erupts in jubilation, and Tony's teammates swarm him in joy. Although he is careful to tell reporters that the victory was "a team effort," Tony is more than happy to take credit for the outcome in his own mind, attributing it to his intelligence and skill as a basketball player.

On the other hand, suppose Tony misses. The buzzer sounds, the crowd groans, and Alain throws up his hands in disbelief, shouting, "I was open!" In the locker room, the coach scolds Tony for his selfishness, accusing him of seeking personal glory rather than making the smarter choice to pass. In this case, Tony is likely to make excuses for his choice, saying that he was only following the coach's instructions, or that Alain might also have missed the shot. He wants to deny responsibility for what happened. The next day, though, Tony's teammates, the newspapers, and the fan discussion boards agree: the loss was Tony's fault. He made a (seemingly defective) choice and must be held accountable.

It's important to distinguish here between *decisions*— however they are made—and the *consequences* of those decisions. We often conflate these when we think about our choices in retrospect. For example, if Tony makes his long shot, he is likely to attribute his success to his (obviously correct!) choice to take the shot. If he misses, he is likely to deny responsibility for his decision to shoot, placing the blame on the confusion of the moment, or his coach's poorly diagrammed play. In other words, Tony's attribution for his shot—his explanation of what caused it—will tend to vary depending on the result. (In psychology, this is called self-serving bias.)

Still, Tony could also do something very courageous after missing the shot: he could accept blame, apologize to his teammates, and promise to try to do better in the future. Over the rest of the season, he could work hard to be a more generous teammate. This is yet another decision that Tony must make on his own. Or is it? Maybe this decision, too, is really determined by forces outside Tony's knowledge and control. Even if Tony does the "right" thing, maybe he deserves no credit for it.

❧

To address these sorts of conundrums, we need a philosophical perspective. In his groundbreaking 2019 book *Why Free*

Will Is Real, the philosopher Christian List argued that free will requires just three related capacities, all operating within humans (and perhaps even robots and other artificially intelligent systems): (1) the capacity to consider several possibilities for action; (2) the capacity to form an intention to pursue one of those possibilities; and (3) the capacity to take action to move toward that possibility.[1] These capacities give an agent the capacity to weigh options at crucial points, to select preferred options, and to work toward them. List argued that psychological research has already shown that these three capacities exist—and indeed, that human behavior can't be understood without assuming that they are operative. (As a psychologist who studies goals and intentions, I agree.)

According to List's theory, our basketball player, Tony, was definitely exercising free will. With three seconds left in the game, he weighs the alternatives (Shoot? Pass? Take a couple more dribbles?), makes a choice (suppose it's "I'll shoot!"), then begins to enact it by launching his body into the air for the shot. The credit—or the blame—for taking the shot belongs to Tony himself.

Step back a second, though, and the picture becomes blurry. For Tony to take the shot, his brain had to send a signal to his muscle fibers to contract, pushing the ball into the air. That neurological signal relied on a complex array of electrical and chemical processes, which in turn relied on trillions of cells in Tony's body and the atoms that make them up—Tony had nothing to do with all that. Even more, Tony doesn't know why he "chose" to shoot in the first place, and doesn't know anything about the brain processes that tipped his decision in that direction. Where is Tony in all of this, and what does it mean for "Tony" to decide? Who (or what) *is* Tony, anyway?

In 1949 the philosopher Gilbert Ryle described the mysterious psychological entity that somehow haunts our merely physical brains.[2] He called this entity "the ghost in the machine" and argued that it is only fictional. In my field of personality psychology, we have a different term for the ghost: we call it the "symbolic self." The symbolic self refers to our sense of ourselves as self-aware agents living a story, playing our roles in the world, and deciding what to do and say next. The symbolic self likely arose after the invention of language, which required humans to evolve the cognitive capacity to create and inhabit a social character living among other characters. The symbolic self is indeed a fiction, just like the ghost in the machine; but it is also *us*—who we feel ourselves to be as we walk through the world making decisions and running our lives. As we'll see, our symbolic selves are riding the very "top level" of our brain's activity, supported by countless neuronal processes below. But we ghosts aren't just helpless: we're choosing where next to ride, affecting everything that happens down in the neurons.

Ryle traced the idea of the ghost in the machine as far back as René Descartes's famous statement "Cogito ergo sum": I think therefore I am. Back in 1637, this was Descartes's way of establishing ground for philosophical inquiry amid radical doubt. Considering the possibility that reality, as he encountered it, was perhaps an illusion crafted by an evil demon (today, we might think of this as a kind of computer simulation), Descartes argued that one fact really is beyond all doubt: there must be a thinker first before there can be doubt about the reality of that thinker. There is a compelling logic to this idea, and I have a little sign hanging in my study that contains my own favorite version: "I doubt, therefore I might be" (ponder that!). Still, by privileging his own internal perspective as the one reliable truth, regardless of what his bodily senses were telling him, Descartes seemed to embrace dualism. Dualism is a theoretical perspective that cleaves the subjective mind from the physical body—hence Ryle's ghost in the machine, in which mind (the ghost) is separate from the physical machine it inhabits.

Dualism remains a very controversial idea within philosophy, and it raises questions about whether the mind can exist without the body, whether there exists a metaphysical soul that somehow becomes joined with the physical body at birth, and whether that soul can somehow survive death or even reconnect with a Supreme Being. To all of these questions, I, like most other scientists, answer "probably not"—although there's no way to know for sure. Nevertheless, I'll argue that as symbolic selves we really *do* have a kind of dualistic separation from our bodies, and that this separation gives us great creative power and a huge degree of freedom to act. We'll consider the nature of this fascinating dualism throughout this book as we consider how to embrace and nurture our inner ghosts and their choice-making capacities rather than discarding or disbelieving in them.

Christian List's theory of free will offers a strong philosophical case for doing just this—for embracing our power of choice. But his theory is also incomplete, from the point of view of psychology. For one, it doesn't tell us how the choice-making architecture actually works. When faced with a decision, how exactly do we call up various options, and then how do we decide between them? List's theory is also silent about the broader context of decision-making. To what extent are we able to choose freely when we're constrained by so many social pressures and other outside influences? Finally, his theory doesn't address the question of *wise* choice—how can we know that we are choosing well?

These are all questions that my field of personality psychology is uniquely equipped to answer, and in my thirty-five-year research career I've collected and published data on all of them. My work focuses on the self-stated personal goals that people report—that is, the broad objectives they are pursuing in life, from what career they'll try to enter and what values they'll uphold to what exercise targets they'll try to hit. My work also focuses on happiness and how we can achieve it.

What I've found is that setting new goals—and then achieving them—is one of the very best paths to happiness and well-being. At any moment, we can decide to adopt a new purpose, course, or aim, and these decisions can potentially change everything, leading to major improvements in our lives. Of course, not all of our goals are portentous and life changing. Nor are we always successful at achieving them. No matter: the point is that, moment to moment, we're constantly selecting just one of the many possibilities in front of us, taking actions that divert the universe into a particular course that never would have happened otherwise. Making choices between imagined alternatives might even be the most profound capacity of human brains—the one that continually "collapses the wave function" of quantum indeterminacy, by launching our physical bodies in one direction or another.[3]

My research on the goals people set for themselves is a big part of my broader quest to understand what I call "optimal human being": how we should live in order to maximize our potential for love, success, creativity, and fulfillment.[4] In pursuing this quest, I've studied many interrelated questions in psychology, including the meaning of freedom, responsibility, and authenticity; how we form intentions, set goals, and develop values; how we can become more integrated and self-actualized individuals; and how all of this affects our personal happiness and sense of well-being. In doing so, I've drawn on approaches from many subdisciplines within psychology, including motivation psychology, positive psychology, personality psychology, social psychology, and decision psychology.

Although all of these disciplines explore somewhat different issues and use different methods, they are all interested in "optimal functioning." Motivation psychology tries to help people get what they want, putting them more in charge of their own destinies. Positive psychology tries to advise people, via experimental research, about activities and practices that could help them grow in beneficial ways. Personality psychology tries to help people become more self-aware and improve the internal coordination of the many cognitive and emotional systems that make up a whole individual. Social psychology tries to tell people how to improve communication with others, how to persuade people to their views, and how to watch out for social pitfalls. Decision psychology tries to help people think more rationally about the choices in front of them, thereby improving the "utility" of their decisions.

Despite the wide variety of approaches among these disciplines, there is one assumption that they all hold in common: that *humans are constantly making choices, for better or worse.* We can't help it—even waiting to choose, or not choosing at all, are choices. These fields also assume that people can learn to make better choices over time—by trying to gather more information, by attending mindfully to their inner states, by noticing and attempting to correct for their biases, by analyzing their strategic mistakes, and much more. When researchers in these fields succeed in their jobs, people gain new tools for improving their lives—and they are better able to take control of them.

This observation leads to a fascinating fact: that *all* major theories of personality development, from Sigmund Freud to Carl Jung to Abraham Maslow to most of my colleagues today, emphasize the importance of becoming more *autonomous* over time—of developing a stronger sense of being a choice-making agent, a stronger sense of being self-determined, a stronger sense of exercising free will. We'll talk more about these theories later, but what this commonality shows is that the question of "whether we have free will" isn't just a matter for the philosophy seminar room. It's a profoundly personal issue that's important for each of us as individuals—because a belief in our own capacity to make free choices, and to learn to make better choices over time, is necessary to become a fully functioning human being.

Why is autonomy—that is, the sense of acting freely—the primary driver of personal growth? In the simplest terms:

because autonomy helps us, as symbolic selves, to run our lives better. Psychological autonomy helps us recognize what we really want, and then to go after it. But at the same time, it helps us to regulate and control ourselves, and even, when necessary, to get ourselves to do things we hate doing. Psychological autonomy helps us to communicate effectively with others, so that they will help and support us. But at the same time, it helps us to care about other people, because it helps us to recognize ourselves in them. In psychologist Roy Baumeister's words, psychological autonomy helps people pursue their "enlightened self-interest" while at the same time adopting (and adapting to) the values and norms of the broader culture.[5]

It has become fashionable for some psychologists to downplay the role of the conscious self, describing it as powerless or clueless. They try to tell us that we're just passive voices in our own heads, only commenting after the fact, with no real power to affect anything. Or that we're easily manipulated and controlled by the social forces around us, in many cases without our awareness. Or that our pretensions to morality are just that—pretensions, easily punctured. Or that we suffer from an inflated sense of self-importance and are afflicted with countless self-serving biases.

These four statements are often true. But *just* as true is the premise of this book: that as symbolic selves we are "driving the car," despite all our flaws and foibles. Human brain functioning is the most complex process in the known universe, and it's the process that we, as symbolic selves, are orchestrating—we are deciding "on the fly"; we continually choose our own way forward despite sometimes grave levels of ignorance; and we do this in ways that no scientific theory, data, or statistical model could ever predict in advance, no matter how sophisticated. We need to educate and strengthen our symbolic selves, not undermine or banish them. They are all that we have.

If free will is real—and even inescapable—then why do we sometimes feel so *un*free? That is, why do we so often feel pushed around by the stress of work, the press of relationships, the strain of discrimination, the mess of politics, and much more? Today, the world seems caught in an escalating psychological crisis: we don't know what's true anymore, we hate people of opposite political stripes, and our towns are burning or flooding as the climate heats up. Are all these problems due merely to our failure to believe that we're free?

Of course not—obviously, these are objective problems, over which we (individually) have little or no control; and, just as obviously, we are entangled in many other such problems besides, both in our own lives and in the world at large. Nevertheless, we often fail to recognize how much choice we actually *do* have, despite all the problems. Thus we may dither and procrastinate, or fail to make decisions altogether. And as a result, we may fail to solve the problems—and fail to turn them into opportunities.

There are many reasons we may not take full advantage of our free will, reasons why we may settle for less than what is possible. Perhaps we have been used and abused by authorities in our lives who have convinced us that they, not we, are in charge. Perhaps our beliefs about ourselves or the world—or even a belief in determinism—block our view forward. Or maybe we live in crushing poverty, or we're part of a minority, discriminated against by the majority. Maybe we live in a society plagued by corruption, strife, and disorder—an increasingly common circumstance in the world today.

But there's another barrier to acting autonomously that shouldn't escape us: sometimes, we may give up our free will on purpose. We try to *avoid* choosing, or we procrastinate. Or, like Tony, after missing the shot, we make excuses, to try to avoid accepting blame for our choices. In these cases, maybe our problem isn't that we have too little freedom, but that we have too *much*—so much that it is scary. What if we choose wrongly, and get into trouble, or have regrets? Like Tony, we are held responsible for our choices (with some legal and medical exceptions), and those choices have the potential to cause suffering, for ourselves or others, or to elicit blame from others. And we might not be able to achieve our cherished goals, and end up feeling bitter disappointment.

Consider a new college student who feels daunted by the dozens of possible academic majors (or friends, or suitors) from which to choose—knowing that these choices may strongly influence the future course of her life. She also must make her selections with far too little knowledge of herself—she's only eighteen. How can she know if she'll still want to be a doctor when she's forty, rather than a dentist, or a designer? Maybe it's easier to just "fall in with the crowd," and do what other people are doing. This cautious attitude makes a certain degree of sense. People are generally unaware of their own nonconscious motivations, and often bad at forecasting how they'll feel about their choices (or non-choices) down the road.

And they often must make decisions without knowing what obstacles and difficulties they will face en route to achieving their selected goals. Perhaps it is better not to have tried, than to have tried and failed.

Because of such dilemmas, people may try to "escape from freedom," to borrow a phrase from the twentieth-century psychiatrist Erich Fromm, whose book by that title explored the psychosocial conditions that enabled the rise of Nazism. Chief among these was the fear of freedom, which contemporaneous existential philosophers singled out as perhaps the most important problem for human beings. The French philosopher Jean-Paul Sartre wrote that we are radically free and "doomed to choose" (and to thereby define ourselves), whether we like it or not.[6] Some people don't like this very much at all, and so they look for something, anything, to feel determined by— including rigid and unbreakable routines, harsh authoritarian leaders, and perhaps theories that deny their free will. But again, even choosing *not* to choose is a choice, according to Sartre's existential perspective. So is choosing not to believe in choice at all.

This book argues that we *always* have free will, at least in the sense that Christian List proposed: we're free to conjure up multiple alternatives, choose one of them, and start moving. In a similar vein, Viktor Frankl, a Nazi prison camp survivor and psychiatrist, felt deeply that we always have the capacity to choose our response to circumstances, no matter how bad they are (and for Frankl, who barely survived his captivity, they were horrendous). In his book *Man's Search for Meaning*, Frankl wrote, "Everything can be taken from a man but one thing: the last of the human freedoms—to choose one's attitude in any given set of circumstances, to choose one's own way."[7]

Yet even those of us who face more mundane challenges than Frankl's may not yet be mature enough, brave enough, or insightful or strong enough to grasp this freedom. Thus the more complicated answer to the question of whether we have free will is that *we're only as free as we think we are.* We can limit our own freedom by believing that we have no freedom—that we have no choice in what we do—and, as we'll see, such beliefs tend to become self-fulfilling prophecies. But tendencies are not certainties: prophecies can fail, and pressures can be resisted. Frankl argued that, as we can't avoid choosing, we might as well find the courage to choose what is important and meaningful. In this book, I'll explore some ways that we can do just that.

CHAPTER 1

THE PROBLEMS WITH DETERMINISM

The philosopher and neuroscientist Sam Harris began his 2012 book *Free Will* (which really argues for hard determinism) with the story of a gruesome crime. In 2007, two men invaded the Connecticut home of William and Jennifer Petit and their two daughters. The men, both career criminals, had apparently broken into the house in order to rob it. But once in the house, the plan shifted. One of the men bludgeoned the father; the other raped and strangled the mother. They then set fire to the house, killing the two daughters.[1] Harris tells this story in service of a radical (some might say disturbing) argument: the killers couldn't have chosen otherwise than to kill the family whose house they invaded. Their behavior was fully determined, and hence would have been completely predictable in advance, given enough knowledge of their underlying history and conditions. Harris also made this striking statement: that if he (Harris) were swapped "atom for atom" with one of the killers, he also couldn't have chosen otherwise—Harris would have been in the grip of the very same murderous compulsion.

At first glance this idea might seem plausible (except for the "swapping atoms" part). The killers were swept along in a chain of events that, in retrospect, seemed to lead inexorably to tragedy. Indeed, the men later described their actions in much this way. But does it really make sense to say the killers were *always* doomed to do what they did, and could not *possibly* have prevented themselves from doing it? This seems to imply predetermination—the doctrine that whatever happens was doomed to happen, since the beginning of time. This is an idea very few scientists endorse, because it requires believing that every future event, everywhere in the universe, was already set in stone at the very moment of the Big Bang fourteen billion years ago. We'll critique this idea more carefully in the next chapter.

Seemingly more plausible is that at every moment, there are many possible things that could happen next—many degrees of freedom in how things turn out. The killers may not have had infinite choices after breaking into the house, but neither did they have just one. If that had been the case—if they really had no degrees of freedom, no ability to consider alternatives (as required in Christian List's model of free will)—then they shouldn't be held legally responsible for their actions. If objective evidence showed organic brain disease or severe mental illness, they would have to be acquitted by reason of insanity.

But Harris presented no evidence that either of the killers was unable to control himself, except for the awfulness of their crimes. Why not instead suppose that the killers had a choice, and made a bad one? Maybe they failed to suppress momentary impulses, failed to think through the likely future consequences of their actions, failed to keep in mind their initial intentions not to hurt anybody during the robbery—and before they knew it, things got out of hand. Next time, if they got another chance, maybe they could do better.

In the next section of this chapter I'll evaluate some of the main assumptions of determinism, showing how implausible, and even hyperbolic, they are. They turn us all into brain-damaged killers![2] Because I am not a philosopher, I will not try to convey the countless subtleties of these long-running debates, about which hundreds of books and thousands of articles have already been written. Nor will I cover the dozens of specific positions on free will that different philosophers have staked out. That would take a whole book in itself. My goal here is only to provide an overall sense of the main scientific arguments for determinism while also providing a common-sense evaluation of those arguments. Maybe the starting assumptions of determinism can at least be questioned, even if they can't be disproven. Establishing such doubt might give us more space in which to think about other possibilities. It would also suggest that people shouldn't succumb to fatalism just yet.

Then, in the second part of the chapter, I'll consider a practical problem with the doctrine of determinism—namely, that believing in it tends to make people less competent, less happy, and less moral. As we'll see, experiments show that convincing people to believe in determinism negatively affects them in many ways. The results of these experiments provide yet more reason for doubt, and reason to pause, on the road to fatalism.

~⊃

According to Christian List, anti-free-will arguments take three basic forms. Here I follow his lead while focusing a bit more on the relevant psychology. I'll call these arguments the "three horsemen" of determinism.

The first horseman is the reductionist (or materialist) perspective, which asserts that there is nothing but matter obeying physical laws. In this view, the only possible correct explanations for human behavior (ultimately) must be physical ones—not biological explanations, and certainly not mental or subjective explanations. Why am I typing this sentence right now? Because a kajillion atomic processes are making it happen. In principle, says the radical reductionist, we should always be able to "reduce" behavior to events taking place all the way down, at the atomic level, to our most basic building blocks. Only there will we find the true causes of our actions.

The reductionist argument is appealing, because it seems intuitively obvious that in reality, everything is built on physics. Of course all events are based on atomic processes, we might say, and are thus explainable by the laws that govern atomic processes. And of course this includes mental events, in which we might think (incorrectly) that "we" are the ones doing the thinking.

But there is an important implication of reductionism that shouldn't go unexamined: that ultimately, the only science we need is physics. Thus, the entire field of biology might become irrelevant because all biological explanations could eventually be replaced by physical explanations. Similarly, the entire field of neuroscience might become irrelevant, because all neurological explanations could come down to biological and then physical explanations. Sam Harris, who is a neuroscientist, says that all of our choices (not just the killers' choices) are determined by microlevel brain processes, emphasizing the biology, but Harris's claim is vulnerable itself to being "reduced down" to even more basic and elementary processes at the molecular, atomic, and quantum levels, the domain of physicists, which might render his field of neuroscience irrelevant. A hard line physicist might say, "Sorry, Sam, brain processes are really nothing more than cellular processes, which are really nothing more than chemical and atomic processes—in the end, you'll have to give up your perspective and join us physicists down here."

In short, a serious problem for reductionism is that there is nowhere to stop before reaching the very bottom level of matter. Any science (or scientific explanation) that relies on anything besides atomic processes is doomed to become obsolete, in the end—they're all just way stations on the road to something truer.

Yet the real truth is that when it comes to understanding and predicting complex human behavior, this sort of reductionism provides almost no useful information. Why? Because the basic building blocks of matter are so far away from the action. Here's an illuminating analogy. In his 1987 book *The Blind Watchmaker*, Richard Dawkins wrote, "The behavior of a motorcar is explained in terms of cylinders, carburetors, and sparking plugs. It is true that each one of these components rests atop a pyramid of explanations at lower levels. But if you asked me how a motorcar worked you would think me somewhat pompous if I answered in terms of Newton's laws and the laws of thermodynamics, and downright obscurantist if I answered in terms of fundamental particles."[3] In other words, to explain the workings of a motorcar, we wouldn't usually resort to physics and chemistry. Instead, we would focus on the mechanical systems of the car—its internal combustion, its steering, its braking, and so on.

But notice that this is only a description of the car's workings—*how* it does what it does. It still doesn't tell us anything about *where* the car goes—its behavior. To understand that, it seems we need to look higher up, not lower down—to the intentions of the person driving the car. When I pull out onto Interstate 70 from my town of Columbia, Missouri, my car either goes left, toward Kansas City, or right, toward St. Louis—but my car's path depends on where *I* want to go, not on anything about the car itself (as long as the car is running). It seems that mental events (that is, our intentions) might have effects that are somehow more than the microlevel physical events that constitute them.

We'll consider this "something more" further in the next chapter. Fully evaluating the problems with reductionism will take additional work. For now, let's turn to the second horseman of determinism.

The second major type of argument against free will comes from the doctrine of predetermination. It says that things couldn't possibly have turned out differently than they did; the universe is a giant machine, clanking along toward an inevitable conclusion. This idea goes back at least to the French scientist Pierre Laplace, who in the late 1700s said that, given complete knowledge of the current configuration of the universe, scientists could perfectly predict every future event just by applying Isaac Newton's laws of motion. And if everything is really predetermined, then we never have a choice about anything. You were always going to find yourself reading this sentence right now, just as I was always going to write it.

This is a hard argument to beat, certainly from a retrospective point of view. After all, it is always the case that only one sequence of events happened in the past. How could it possibly have been otherwise? My dad has said this many times.

But as scientists, we are in the business of predicting (knowing in advance), not post-dicting (explaining after the fact). Predicting complex human behavior is much more difficult, I assure you, than explaining it after the fact. It's relatively easy to concoct a post hoc story about what happened and why. It's much harder (and maybe even impossible) to predict what will happen before it happens. For example, if we wanted to predict whether a person was likely to get vaccinated for a particular illness, we might create a statistical model that took into account demographic information (age, location, and so on) and measurements of certain beliefs (trust in the health-care system and the like). Our model might predict that an older person in an urban area is more likely to get vaccinated than a younger person in the same urban area, or a rural older adult. But never does a model of this sort—even a very complex one that takes in all sorts of data—manage to predict human behavior with 100 percent accuracy. There are always exceptions, and often, scientists are lucky to get more than 50 percent accuracy—and that's only if they include people's measured intentions in the model. (Are they *planning* to get vaccinated, yes or no?) If individual behavior really was predetermined, you'd think that by now scientists would be better at predicting it in advance.

A determinist might argue that this is just a data problem. As our research methodologies and data analysis capabilities improve, we'll get better and better at predicting in advance what will happen.

This is undeniably true—additional information always reduces prediction error. For example, if we take measurements of the *other people* in a person's environment, in addition to taking measurements of the person, then we'll be in a better position to predict whether that person will get vaccinated (and, not surprisingly, research shows people are less likely to get vaccinated if their families are against it). Still, I contend that much of the variation in what people do will *never* be predictable in advance, because the determination of the next moment often happens just at the cusp of the moment before it, as influenced by the newly ascertained set of possibilities called forth within a person's mind at that moment of decision, as that person makes a subjective choice among those possibilities. Furthermore, our choices are always deeply entwined in the momentary situations in which we find ourselves—our situations are as unique as we are. But scientists are still far from being able to predict what precise situations people will encounter at every moment. How could people's *responses* to situations be predicted in advance if we can't even tell what their *situations* will be?

Another problem with the doctrine of predetermination, similar to reductionism's problem that there is nowhere to stop before the bottom, is that there is nowhere to stop as one goes backward in time—the chain must ultimately be traced back to the conditions at the birth of the universe (presumably in a big bang). In other words, if every event is predetermined, then the causes that determined that event were also predetermined, and so on and so on, all the way back to the very beginning.

But surely no entity, scientific or deistic, could possibly have known, way back at the very first moment of our universe (if they somehow had a window seat), everything that would occur at every moment, everywhere in the universe, through all the billions of years of its existence. This would only make sense if our universe were an experiment with precise starting conditions that had been "run" many times before by some uber-powerful alien being—an experiment that always turned out exactly the same way. The Book of Genesis describes just such an experiment being run—although theologians disagree on whether God knows everything in advance. Maybe He didn't know and was curious to find out what we would do. But it seems rather implausible that such godlike beings, and such experiments, could exist—and, in any case, they would be impossible to approach scientifically.

A more commonsense perspective, the one we live by, is that there are nearly infinite contingencies and degrees of freedom in this complex universe, and thus many different ways things could turn out. A random momentary event—a stray breeze, a chance remark, an odd coincidence—may kick off a chain of events leading to radically different outcomes than would have otherwise been expected. In chaos theory this is

called "the butterfly effect," in which the tiny flap of a butterfly's wing in, say, South America may ultimately determine
a major weather event in a distant location, such as North
America.[4]

But maybe the idea of predetermination can handle this.
A weaker version of the doctrine holds that random (and thus
unpredictable) processes, in addition to lawfully regulated
(thus predictable) processes, also affect what happens. This
view admits that we may never be able to predict everything in
advance, but says it is only because there is some randomness
in the system—not because intentional agents (such as ourselves) intervene or make choices that have effects. According
to this view, to the extent that humans behave unpredictably,
it is only because they act randomly—not because they act
purposefully.

But, possibly, neither predetermination nor random determination can adequately describe what is actually happening in human lives. We don't choose the situations in which
we find ourselves (though our predecessor selves often had
influence on those situations, via our prior decisions), nor do
we choose to have the perceptions we have of the situations,
nor do we directly produce the list of possible behavioral responses that we call forth from our nonconscious minds. In
the determinist perspective, all of these facts are said to nul-
lify the possibility of free will—only omniscient (all-knowing)
free will counts.

But maybe our merely finite self-knowledge doesn't matter; maybe what matters is that we, as "selves of the moment,"
take what we find (as Tony did with three seconds left in the

game), and then decide what we want to do next ("I'll shoot!" versus "I'll pass"). We impose our purposes upon the world. In Christian List's terminology, we have the perhaps inalienable capacity, at every moment, to consider alternatives, form intentions, and take action. From this perspective, we're neither predetermined nor random—instead, we're biased, in favor of our wants, needs, and desires, as best as we can perceive these, at the moment of decision.

It's true that we may not be able to perceive our own needs and wants clearly and may not know what to choose. But this seems to turn the problem of free will into a different problem: of how to use free will wisely. And perhaps we can answer this question with science.

The third horseman of determinism is epiphenomenalism. According to the *Oxford English Dictionary*, an epiphenomenon is "a secondary effect or byproduct that arises from but does not causally influence a process." That is, it is a mere side effect, like the noise produced by a vacuum cleaner, or the smoke produced by a fire. Noise and smoke don't *cause* the events that create them; they are just symptoms of those events. In the epiphenomenal view, our experiences are always mere symptoms of prior causes; they are never causes themselves. They're dead ends in the chain.

From the epiphenomenal perspective, our feelings of being intentional agents are delusional. As in the reductionist perspective, this view says that scientists may someday be able to predict human behavior, but only via a thorough understanding of physics and chemistry, and maybe molecular biology, and, just possibly, neuroscience. There will be no need, once physical, biological, and neuroscience research theories and data are sufficiently advanced, for researchers to consider what people are thinking, feeling, or intending to do—these are just epiphenomenal side effects that don't actually have any influence on our behavior.

Sam Harris's book *Free Will* primarily adopted the reductionist and epiphenomenalist objections to free will, which makes sense, given that Harris is a neuroscientist. Neuroscientists tend to assume that all behaviors can be explained by physical brain processes that occur beneath our awareness. Presumably, Harris would have to admit that his decision to write his own book, and even his fervent belief in determinism, were caused by factors beyond his control (but then, why is he so sure he's right?).[5] But I would argue that Harris *was* in control of his decision to write *Free Will*: he liked the idea of determinism, as he thought about it, and thus, he made the choice to write a book in support of it.

Harris's book is largely an elaboration of the epiphenomenal implications of a famous set of experimental studies conducted by the neuroscientist Benjamin Libet and his colleagues.[6] In such experiments, participants are seated in front of a clock and asked to push a button at some moment of their choosing. When they decide to push the button, they mentally note the exact time on the clock in order to report it later to the researchers.

Libet found that a measurable action potential (that is, an electric impulse in the neurons responsible for moving the hand that pressed the button) began within participants' brains before the moment the participants experienced deciding—sometimes a full second before. Brain activity apparently comes first, then the subjective sense of choice. The implication was that participants' microlevel neural processes caused the button-pushing, not their felt decisions to push the button. The experience of deciding may simply have been an epiphenomenon, a phenomenon that only came after the critical neural processes, just as smoke comes only after a fire starts, and can never start the fire.

There have been many critiques of this interpretation of Libet's results, on both methodological and logical grounds.[7] However, even if Libet's results are interpreted exactly as described above, they still do not rule out the possibility that our subjective intentions matter.

First, as we'll see in the next chapter, higher-level and more complex mental processes always occur more slowly than lower-level ones, because they involve integration across more of those lower-level processes. But so what—wouldn't we want the mental executive to come last, after the information is in, when the time has come for decisions to be made? Libet himself endorsed this idea, saying that conscious processes retain veto power, if nothing else—"Free won't," as he cleverly termed it. We can decide *not* to do what we were about to do. We can decide not to press the button—or make the snarky remark or open the bag of potato chips. In 2019, Marcel Brass, Ariel Furstenberg, and Alfred Mele (a brain scientist, a psychologist, and a philosopher) similarly concluded that the Libet experiments don't discount free will, in part because "the decision process is configured by conditional intentions that participants form at the beginning of the experiment."[8]

Participants in Libet's experiments start out with an intention to push the button at a certain time of their own choosing, then delegate their brains to pick a particular moment; thus they arrive at the place they set themselves into motion to go. Yes, nonconscious processes in their brains help them get there; but their prior intentions started those nonconscious processes going.

Here's a personal example of such "self-conditioning," in which my own prior decision biases my brain in a particular direction. I play tennis, and often find myself in a situation in which I'm not sure where I'll direct my next shot. I don't make the decision until the instant I begin to swing my racket (by then I have no choice but to decide). I believe that no scientific data or model could flawlessly predict what decision I will make at every such moment, no matter how much data it had. I certainly couldn't do it (unless I cheated and just did whatever I said I would do), and neither could anybody else. Why? Because my decision is informed by my tennis mind's best estimation, at that exact moment, of the right strategy—on that day ("I planned to work on my short drop shots today"), at that stage of the match ("It's an important point in a deciding game"), against that opponent ("He's faster side to side than back to front"). And my decision is informed by the unfolding logic of the point-as-played, in which I have perhaps maneuvered my opponent into a vulnerable position that I can exploit ("He's behind the baseline, and I know he's getting tired"). My final decision ("Perfect time to try a short drop shot!") is the output of a momentary integrative process that is unique to me and to that moment. It is also unique to that day, given my own prior intention to work on my drop shots that day (self-conditioning). Of course, my short shot might fail to clear the net. Again, decisions, and the results of decisions, are two separate things.

If a neuroscientist wants to claim that my "drop shot decision" was predetermined by, and fully predictable from, complete knowledge of my prior history and current brain-state, they'll have to show me the data. But they have no such data, and never will. So far, the reductionist argument is mainly a promissory argument, more like an article of scientific faith than a demonstrated fact. The same is true for the epiphenomenon argument, which ultimately relies on the same assumption—that if you had complete knowledge of the microlevel processes going on inside the person, you could make perfect predictions. I think it's important to keep this in mind.

To some, this whole debate might seem empty and pointless. Even if our actions and thoughts are determined, we mostly don't feel it: we think about possibilities, weigh alternatives, make choices, create and adjust plans, and try to learn from our mistakes. In other words, even if determinism were correct, it probably wouldn't affect our everyday lives. So why not just accept it? After all, science has explained so much, and it continues to explain more every day. Why not just admit that someday, science will be able to perfectly predict what we will do in advance? As a scientist who conducts studies to try to predict behavior, studies which always have a lot of error, I see how this idea could be appealing!

But there's at least one big reason not to agree that determinism "must be true": namely, that accepting determinism might have grave costs for people's lives and functioning, inducing a sense of fatalism and resignation. What is the good of thinking carefully, of expending effort, of trying to be a good person, if we aren't responsible for—and can't even affect—how things turn out? If everything is predetermined, why not just coast? Suppose we convinced people that they had no control over any of their actions—that at no point in their lives could they have made different decisions than the ones they made. If they accepted this as true, then why should they even try to say no to snarky remarks or bags of chips, or to say yes to bold new life-goals? What if a belief in determinism renders people helpless? Thinkers who endorse and write about determinism sometimes report receiving despairing notes from readers claiming that their lives have been ruined by reading the thinker's work, even to the point of contemplating suicide.

These questions suggest a practical criterion for assessing the value of the determinist ideology that goes beyond the scientific criteria I have just discussed: If people acquire a new belief in determinism, do they gain, or do they suffer? By the logic of scientific progress, they should gain. The clouds have parted, and they have emerged into the light of truth. But if they suffer, perhaps they have adopted incorrect beliefs, beliefs that may now be preventing them from exercising freedoms that are otherwise available to them. The thought "I can't affect anything" can curdle into "I won't try to do anything."

My field of social-personality psychology provides rigorous experimental methods for investigating just such questions.

In 2008, Kathleen Vohs and Jonathan Schooler published a set of experiments that clearly demonstrated the harmful effects of convincing people that determinism is real.[9] In the determinism condition, participants started by reading a short article claiming (in brief) that "rational, high-minded people, and almost all scientists, now recognize that actual free will is an illusion. Why do we have this illusion? It is a mere consequence of our mental architecture." In the control condition, participants instead read an article on the murky topic of consciousness, which didn't mention the free-will issue. Then, participants in both conditions rated their general sense of free will at that moment, using an established measure of this belief. Finally, they were asked to take a test of their math skills in a carefully contrived situation where they could cheat if they chose to do so. The finding: participants who read the article about determinism cheated more on the test than those who read about consciousness in general. Why should they try to be moral, and resist the temptation to cheat, if their sense of making the difficult moral choice is a mere delusion? They might as well take what they can get.

Even more interesting: the cheating behavior of participants in the determinism condition could be statistically explained by their weaker belief in free will, as measured after they read the passage. In other words, participants in the determinism condition tended to believe what they read, and those lower measured beliefs in free will in turn predicted greater cheating. A leads to B leads to C.

In a second experiment, Vohs and Schooler manipulated participants' beliefs in a different way. Participants read fifteen statements and thought about each statement for one minute. In the free-will condition, all fifteen statements asserted that people have the capacity for self-regulation, such as, "I am able to override the genetic and environmental factors that sometimes influence my behavior." In the determinism condition, all fifteen statements denied the capacity for free will: "A belief in free will contradicts the known fact that the universe is governed by lawful principles of science." There was also a third, neutral control condition in which participants read factual statements, such as "Sugar cane and sugar beets are grown in 112 countries."

Participants were then given questions similar to those on the Graduate Record Examination (GRE), the admissions test for graduate school, and told they would receive one dollar for each problem they solved correctly. Yet again, cheating was an option: participants were (supposedly anonymously) allowed to score their answers themselves, then take the money due them and walk away. Participants in the determinism condition walked away with more money than those in the free-will condition, and not because they solved more problems correctly. As in the first study, these differences in cheating behavior were statistically explained by the fact that participants in the determinism condition had lost their belief in free will.

In 2009, psychologists Roy Baumeister, E. J. Masicampo, and C. Nathan DeWall used the same methodology to further explore the negative effects of a belief in determinism.[10] In their first experiment, participants in the determinism condition (compared to the free-will condition) said they would be less inclined to help needy others (such as letting a classmate use their cell phone or giving change to a homeless person). In a second experiment, participants were given a subtle opportunity to act aggressively toward an assigned partner in the study, whom they would not meet. In what was described as a "taste preferences" study, participants saw "background" information revealing that their assigned partner didn't like spicy foods. Participants were then asked to assign a particular quantity of hot sauce that their partner would have to consume as part of a taste test. (This is a very commonly used measure in aggression research.) Those in the determinism condition assigned almost twice as much hot sauce to the spice-averse partner (17.8 milligrams, on average, compared to 9.4 milligrams in the free-will condition). Maybe they were just trying to feed the partner? No, there was no difference between the two conditions in the amount of cheese assigned to the partner for tasting. This tells us that participants in the determinism condition indulged a mean-spirited impulse to cause another person's suffering, whereas those in the free-will condition resisted this temptation. Perhaps those in the determinism condition resented being told that they had no control in life, and took it out on their partner. Or perhaps they just felt like it was impossible to resist that urge to be mean.

Numerous other studies have shown similar negative effects of beliefs in determinism, whether measured as a trait (meaning that in general, the person already believes in the doctrine of determinism), or as a state (meaning that the experimenters have just convinced the person of determinism). People who believe, or are led to believe, in determinism expect to have less career success and objectively perform worse in their jobs. They have less ability to resist temptation and to form plans for the future. They have less self-control and less ability to delay gratification. The list goes on and on.

Now, let's put aside the question of whether determinism is correct or not (I hope I've established that the jury is still out—that there's "reasonable doubt" about determinism). Let's now ask, "What is the possible allure of the deterministic belief system, and why might people choose it over other belief systems?" One answer is that to many people, it's obviously true—they can't disbelieve in it any more than they can disbelieve that the world is round, or that $4 + 4 = 8$. That's what my dad would say. But there might also be other factors, processes, or forces at work. What function might this belief serve in determinists' emotional lives? What needs does it meet, or problems does it solve?

One possibility is that it is comforting to think that everything we do is rationally explainable by science (or will be eventually), if not by some spiritual system. Under determinism, there is an order and logic to our behavior, even if we can't understand it. Another possibility is that some people see determinism as the more intelligent position to take. They like seeing themselves as too smart to fall for nonscientific illusions. Or maybe determinism makes life easy: whatever will be, will be. Determinists of this stripe might take a relaxed, laissez-faire attitude toward their lives, and you can't really blame them for that. Or it could just be convenient to think we have no part in how things turn out, especially when things don't turn out well. Here, we're like Tony: if we've just missed the game-deciding shot, determinism lets us off the hook of responsibility.

Yet there are dangers to such beliefs. As we've seen, people convinced by experiments that determinism is real and free will isn't become more pessimistic and helpless, more ineffective and incompetent, and more amoral and uncaring than those who retain a belief in free will. These experiments suggest that if a belief in determinism is a coping mechanism, or a self-esteem-enhancing strategy, or an effort-avoidance strategy, it's not really working. It may instead be a maladaptive or self-defeating strategy—one that might make us feel better for a while, but disempowers us in the end.

*   *   *

Still, facts are facts, and if determinism is true, and if this fact punctures our illusions—even causing rudeness and despair—so what? Sometimes the truth is painful, but that doesn't make it untrue. Maybe we need to wake up to our merely illusory free will, so we can move beyond it to something better. No wishful thinking, better wrong than ignorant.

To overcome this dilemma, it seems that we need a new way of looking at things—a way that explains logically how mental intentions, insubstantial as they may be, can have legitimate causal effects in the universe. This way of thinking should also explain the role of our symbolic selves—the psychological persons we feel ourselves to be, the ghosts in our own machines. In the next chapter, we'll consider what such a way of thinking might look like.

CHAPTER 2

THE GRAND HIERARCHY OF HUMAN REALITY

Research psychology is a huge field, and it remains split on the free-will question. On the one hand, psychology aims to be (and is) a natural science. That is, psychologists ask questions, form hypotheses, design ways to measure key variables, and then objectively analyze the results. As a science, psychology largely buys into the deterministic approach: "When our theories, methods, and data get good enough, we'll be able to understand everything, and thus predict everything in advance." Objectivity is key because it yields true facts (no wishful thinking allowed; better wrong than ignorant).

On the other hand, psychology is also the science that studies goals, intentions, decision-making, and executive functioning. These are mental processes, imbued with subjectivity, that, once measured, are easily shown to have important effects on people's actions and outcomes in life, as I've found in the course of my own research.

So how does psychology deal with this schism? It depends on the "level of organization" at which the psychologist
works. While psychologists don't go so far as to study atomic
processes like physicists do, those whose work focuses on
the brain—including cognitive neuroscientists such as Sam
Harris—are apt to describe behavior as being determined by
brain-level processes that occur far below awareness. In contrast, psychologists working on personality, emotions, attitudes, and the like (myself included), and largely focusing on
individuals, are more apt to describe behavior as being affected by higher-level mental and subjective processes—the
choices we make, the beliefs we hold, how we regulate ourselves, and so on.

But it doesn't stop there. Social psychologists, who study
interactions between individuals and groups, along with sociologists and anthropologists, who study cultural processes,
could be said to be working at higher levels still. They are inclined to see the main causes of behavior as involving group
rather than individual processes. A social role theorist might
say, for example, that people act in particular ways because it
is in accordance with their defined place in society, not because they make free and conscious choices. And a cultural
anthropologist might claim that behavior can be reduced to
societal programming: "That's what people are conditioned to
do in this kind of culture." It seems that every science relevant
to human behavior wants to claim that it has the best answers.
There is a kind of disciplinary chauvinism, a competition for
attention and funding.

The truth is that all these perspectives have something to contribute. As a researcher in personality science, I know that our decisions, goals, and choices are powerful, and that they can make things occur that wouldn't have occurred otherwise. But our intentions surely don't determine everything. Look how often we forget about them or fail in pursuing them! Also, our mental intentions don't simply float in a vacuum. They are grounded in countless physical processes down in our bodies. And they are influenced by countless social processes out in the world. How can we think about all these factors at once?

Let's start with an undeniable observation: there is nothing in the universe but atoms (and their associated elementary particles). Really—that's all there is! Atoms have long been conceptualized as the building blocks of matter, going back to the ancient Greek thinker Democritus, and this has been confirmed by twentieth-century research. If there are only atoms, then maybe the only science we need is atomic physics.

But seemingly, atoms aren't the end of the story, because atoms are able to combine with each other and form new substances with new properties. Consider the water molecule, which contains two hydrogen atoms and one oxygen atom (H_2O). Unlike the two elements hydrogen and oxygen, water molecules are liquid at temperatures of 0°C–100°C (32°F–212°F) and expand in volume rather than contracting when in a frozen state. To understand these newly emergent properties, we had to develop a new science: chemistry.

So is the story over—are physics and chemistry the only sciences we need in order to understand human behavior?

Alas, seemingly not. In some way that remains mysterious, either on ancient Earth or perhaps on some other planet or comet, molecules became combined with each other in a brand-new way to create living organisms. Living organisms have a great many new properties that go far beyond the properties of the mere chemicals involved—organisms metabolize, grow, and reproduce. To understand these new properties, we had to invent organic chemistry, which studies the new kinds of chemical processes occurring within, and sustaining, living organisms.

But it turns out that living organisms are doing things that organic chemistry alone can't explain—down in their cells, organisms are harnessing and regulating the chemical processes, taking control of them, in ways that benefit the cell. To understand these processes, we needed a new science—microbiology.

You can see where I'm going, so let's cut to the chase. The diagram shown here, adapted from my 2004 book and later writings, illustrates a nested hierarchy of control systems that I call the "grand hierarchy of human reality."[1] The basic idea of this hierarchy is not new. It was first proposed in the nineteenth century by Auguste Comte.[2] It is also endorsed in some form or another by almost all behavioral scientists working today (and most other scientists besides). But when we look at the hierarchy in the context of trying to understand the causes of human behavior, we see that it still has many novel insights to yield.

The Grand Hierarchy

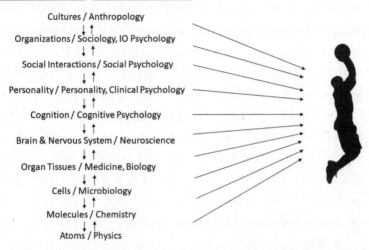

Grand hierarchy of human reality, courtesy of Kennon M. Sheldon

The diagram shows a young man (we called him Tony in the introduction) at a tense moment (time t) in a big game. Immediately before that moment, Tony felt unsure about what to do with the basketball he was holding. But at time t, he decides to take the shot. Why? Is there a way to explain, or better yet, to have predicted in advance, that Tony would take the long shot at time t, rather than passing the ball to a teammate? Imagine—as a scientist—having all the data you could possibly want: every piece of information you could think of that might be relevant in this scenario. To fully model a human being and thereby predict their next behavior with complete accuracy, what would the data set need to look like?

The grand hierarchy provides a framework for answering this question. As the figure shows, there are many different levels of organization that constitute a human being, and these levels can be related to each other via both "top-down" and "bottom-up" effects (represented by the up and down arrows in the diagram). Each level might also influence the causation of a behavior (represented by the horizontal arrows reaching toward Tony's shot).

Obviously, Tony is made up of atoms—that's all there is, remember! But it seems unlikely that we'll ever completely reduce Tony's decision to the measured activity of his atoms (all 5×10^{27} of them). We need more than a single arrow, reaching from the atomic level of organization toward the shooting of the basketball. Yes, Tony couldn't take a shot without the atoms that make him up, but the atoms mainly support and constrain, rather than control, the behavior. It seems that something more complex is doing the controlling, above the atomic level.

This point already illustrates an important general principle about the grand hierarchy: that there is a kind of "functional autonomy" at each new level, which builds upon what is given below. This means that each new level affects the world in a way that is partially independent of the levels below. In other words, higher-level processes are not simply determined by processes at the levels below, although they couldn't happen without those lower-level processes. Instead, higher levels can act downward, to affect what happens down in the lower levels. In philosophical language, chemical processes *entrain* atomic processes—that is, chemical processes *supervene* upon their constituent atomic processes, causing the atoms to do things they otherwise wouldn't have done. Something more complicated is taking control of something less complicated.

One implication of this fact is that at each higher level of organization, a new field of science was required. Again, chemistry is the science that studies molecules and compounds, which are higher-order aggregates built of atoms. Chemical processes can control atomic processes, although chemistry couldn't happen without atoms.

Okay, so Tony is a sack of chemicals. Does that tell us enough to predict whether he will take the shot, or instead pass? Again, no—it seems that even with a complete accounting of the millions of different molecular compounds inside of Tony, and with complete knowledge of all the interactions between all these compounds at time t, we wouldn't get very far. Chemical compounds and molecules tend to move toward entropy—that is, they release their available energy and move downhill toward simpler compounds: they break down. Here, it seems that we must go up to a new kind of organizing process, where complexity is somehow being created, maintained, and even increased: we need to cross the mysterious boundary between nonliving and living matter, between the dead and the quick. We need to think about living cells.

At the most basic level, a human body consists of nothing but cells (approximately thirty-seven trillion of them), just as matter consists of nothing but atoms, at the most basic level of all. Cells each have their own individual existences—they are born, they live, they die. In a very important sense, we are nothing more than giant towers of individual cells, each cell managing to coexist with the other cells, like residents of a huge apartment building.

All right, so Tony is a tower of cells. Could an all-knowing microbiologist, fully informed about every cell's current functioning (how each is taking in nutrition, excreting waste, defending itself, reproducing, and so on), and having data from all thirty-seven trillion cells, have predicted, in advance, that Tony would shoot (or not) at time t? Would just three arrows, leading from atoms, molecules, and cells to the behavior, be enough to complete our diagram?

It still seems doubtful—because of everything else going on at time t. There's a lot happening in Tony's perceptions, thoughts, and emotions; in his interactions with teammates and coaches; in the screaming of the crowd; and in the history of the rivalry between the two universities. It seems we need much more information for any kind of complete model.

At the next level up from microcellular matter we find organ systems, which are macrolevel groups of specialized cell types. Organs allow the multicellular organism to function well as an entire unit. Each organ system, as a whole, does things that it doesn't do when its cells are isolated; together, billions of cells mesh into distinctive machines that accomplish important tasks for the entire body. Bodies contain many types of specialized organ cells, including skin cells, liver cells, bone cells, kidney cells, and muscle cells. To understand what they are doing, we needed to invent new sciences: physiology and medicine.

So Tony is more than a tower of microscopic cells—he is a pile of organs and organ systems. Could full knowledge of the conditions in his organs—his heart, his liver, his bones—explain his decision to shoot? It still seems that something is missing. All but the most primitive animals have a special kind of organ system, called the nervous system. The function of the nervous system is to regulate the other organ systems, so that they work as designed and operate in concert with each other. The central nervous system is a control system. It receives information from the other systems and uses this information to regulate the operation of those subsystems. The autonomic nervous system, for example, regulates critical processes such as breathing, digestion, and alertness, keeping each process within its range of effective functioning and in balance with the others.

The autonomic nervous system is automatic—it operates mechanically, and it could not do other than what it does (although biofeedback research, in which people learn to regulate autonomic processes by getting information about the momentary state of those processes, somewhat calls this into question). During the game, Tony's breathing (boosted), heart rate (boosted), and digestive processes (inhibited) are all being influenced automatically, beneath his awareness. These processes help to explain how Tony can play the game at all. But the autonomic nervous system cannot explain Tony's decision to shoot at time *t*.

It seems we need to turn to the "higher" parts of the brain, such as the cerebral cortex, the seat of thought and planning, to better understand Tony's decision. Tony couldn't have decided anything without a cortex. But did his cortex *make* the decision, or did it merely *support* the decision-making?

The logic of the grand hierarchy suggests the latter. Brains are the hardware in which information processing can take place. But to understand that information processing, we will need to consider it at its own level—specifically, in terms of how people mentally encode the complex waves of information streaming in, how they integrate that information with their existing knowledge and with their current goals and desires, and how they use it to decide what to do next.

Capturing this fact, the next level of organization in the grand hierarchy is cognition—the research domain of cognitive psychology. We have crossed an important threshold here, between brute matter and mysterious mind. But the mind is best viewed not simply as a byproduct of the brain. Instead, the brain provides a computer—the hardware—and the mind is the software that runs the computer. It's sometimes said that "Mind is what the brain does." But what is the mind doing? Running the person's brain, that's what! We are (in part) self-programming organisms.

So: At time $t - 1$, the moment before the event depicted in the diagram, Tony's mind was fully engaged in playing the game—looking for openings, predicting where his teammates would go in the next split second, computing angles and distances, and considering whether to shoot. If Tony was playing well, he computed these things more or less correctly, based on his knowledge of the game of basketball, his assessment of his own shooting ability, and his judgment of the situation in that moment on the court. If he decides to take the shot, it's because all of this somehow comes together such that Tony concludes, correctly, that his shot at time t provides the best chance for his team to win the game.

Here again we see all three of the capacities that Christian List described as constituting free will. An agent is able to consider alternative behavioral possibilities in the moment ("I could shoot, or I could pass it to my teammate who is cutting toward the basket"), is able to form an intention ("I will shoot"), and is able to take action in service of the intention (jumping into the air while propelling the ball away from his body with his arms and hands). A sports psychologist with a cognitive focus could potentially measure each part of the decision process, and input these data into a statistical model developed from experimental and field data, to predict whether Tony will shoot at time t—and the model would be very helpful, much better than a mere guess. A sports psychologist considering the behavior using these measures would be able to do the best job yet at predicting the outcome—certainly better than the atomic physicist or the microbiologist.

Is cognitive psychology as high up the ladder as we need to go? Probably not. Suppose that Tony is a "gunner," prone to shoot at any time, from almost anywhere on the court. According to his coach and teammates, Tony is biased to shoot when he shouldn't, incorrectly concluding that his shot offers the best chance for the team to score on a particular possession. Perhaps he is addicted to the applause he receives when he makes a basket. He could be nursing a grudge against a teammate and want to show him that he's the better player. Or Tony might be arrogant, or a narcissist, unable to accept the fact that he isn't as good as he thinks he is. His dreams of becoming an NBA superstar in the future might also be influencing him in the direction of taking the shot—he thinks that to reach that goal, he must be a superstar now, at his current level, and score in the big moments.

We have arrived at the level of *personality*, which can be defined as the characteristic organization of thoughts, feelings, and motivations within a person. All three of these kinds of mental events can impact a person's decision-making—potentially biasing or distorting decisions, but also potentially focusing and sharpening decisions. Personality processes are the scientific domain of personality psychology, clinical psychology, and psychiatry. I'll talk much more about personality processes in later chapters, since that's where so much of the "action" is in trying to understand what and how people choose.

Notice that we have now crossed several thresholds in the grand hierarchy: from nonliving matter to living matter; from living matter to mind; and from mind to personality. The next level up, concerning interpersonal relations, crosses another very important threshold. Up to this point, the hierarchy describes only the conditions and processes going on inside one person's body, including personality processes at the top. But the social psychologists mentioned at the beginning of this chapter have a point: human beings are social animals, existing within complex networks of relationships with other humans. And these relationships with other bodies (other personalities) can be very much part of the explanation for a particular body's behavior.

For example, Tony has an ongoing relationship with his coach. Suppose his ill-advised shot misses, and then further suppose that the coach scolds him. In the next game, Tony passes instead of shooting in a similar situation. He has learned to function better within the multi-body process in which he is entrained—a university basketball game.

What has caused this change in his decision process?

One possible explanation is that Tony wants to please his coach. Communication from the coach has changed the parameters of Tony's decision-making, leading to a different decision than before. A social psychologist would look at how different personalities exchange information, both verbally and nonverbally; how they negotiate status and resolve conflicts; and how the interpersonal processes affect what happens, for all concerned. Social psychology has been instrumental in helping us understand many phenomena, such as social conformity, cooperation, prejudice, altruism, groupthink, and more.

Still, processes at the social relations level don't necessarily win the day any more than any other level of organization. Some people may be especially hard to influence! Suppose that despite his coach's scolding, in the team's next game Tony still takes a very risky shot—and misses it, prompting an unwanted stint on the bench. Once again it was Tony's choice whether to shoot, and once again he chose poorly. For some reason, Tony was immune to his coach's influence.

This example helps to clarify an important issue. There is a big disconnect between individual bodies and other bodies—and this marks a very important "phase transition" within the grand hierarchy. It means that social forces don't control us directly (although maybe they will someday, if we evolve into some kind of superorganism). Rather, social forces merely *influence* us to some varying degree, via norms, laws, expectations, persuasions, and the like. As we'll see in Chapter 4, those wielding social power sometimes try to make us think we *must* do what they say, trying to take direct control of us. Tony's coach would like Tony to think he has to do what the coach says, especially after Tony makes a bad decision.

Unfortunately, from the coach's point of view, he *can't* take direct control of Tony's choices—they remain Tony's own, no matter what the coach says. The individual decision-maker remains king. Tony remains free (while he is in the game) to ignore his coach's advice, and free to take a risky shot in the next tense moment. Of course, he might pay a price for that decision—maybe he'll even get kicked off the team—but that's his prerogative.

Further up in the hierarchy there are even higher levels of organization: large groups, companies, or institutions. Companies and corporations have their own internal norms and practices, which exert top-down influence upon all the people enmeshed within them. But once again, large groups don't directly control the people within them (a fact that is bemoaned by vaccine hesitancy researchers)—they merely provide incentives or arguments to do what the organizational process has deemed important, which individual choice-makers may follow or ignore (at their own peril). These processes form the research domain of organizational psychologists and sociologists.

Returning to our running example: Tony's team, as noted above, represents a university, and it is competing against another university's team. University-level organizational processes can have many influences upon team-level processes, ranging from the quality of the players recruited to the salary of the coach and the dedication of the fans. Maybe, because of the confluence of these factors, Tony's team almost always wins. But, consistent with the up-pointing arrows in the grand hierarchy, relation- and team-level processes can also have a bottom-up influence on higher levels. If Tony's team is persistently terrible, the university's image will be tarnished, and its athletics program may no longer be able to support itself. Lower-level processes can negatively impact higher-level processes, both within the brain and within the team, especially when they aren't working correctly.

Finally, at the highest level in the diagram, we find culture—very large groups of people who experience long-lasting commonality and communality, often based on ethnicity or geographical borders. As a people, they share cultural traditions, norms, practices, and the like. National governments typically supply the organizational structure, if there is one, within cultures. In a collectivist culture, the player in the diagram might tend to make a different decision than his US counterpart. Perhaps he would be more likely to forgo the opportunity to take the long shot, in order to conform to a status hierarchy, or to promote team harmony. Cultural influences are the scientific domain of cultural anthropologists and cross-cultural psychologists.

*   *   *

I hope you see that to better predict a person's behavior, we need information from all of these levels of organization—which we will have to obtain separately, from each level. Having information about people's mental lives—their intentions in the situation—will help a lot. But even with exhaustive prior information, we may never be able to predict behavior with 100 percent accuracy. It was Tony's final decision, at time t, whether to shoot, just like it is my decision to try drop shots versus lobs at critical moments in my tennis matches. A highly informed observer could predict, with much greater than chance accuracy, what Tony or I might do, but could never know, in advance, with full and final certainty.

In the next chapter we'll develop some conceptual tools for understanding how higher-level processes are able to reach down to affect lower-level processes—and thus, how our mental intentions can have irreducible effects upon the behavior of our bodies. We'll see that we really are "driving the car," for better or worse—that's our function, and we can't help performing it, even if we do it badly.

CHAPTER 3

THE SOURCE OF OUR FREE WILL

Human personality processes occur at a very high level of organization within the physical universe, one that is layered on top of a dazzling array of biological machinery. Conditions in our brain and the rest of our body—contractions in our stomach lining, the release of cortisol into our bloodstream—inform the decisions we make as a symbolic self, telling us that we're hungry or afraid, and spurring us to eat that muffin or back away from that rattlesnake. We call the things the symbolic self does—things such as making a decision or concocting a strategy—personality processes, and as the grand hierarchy would suggest, selves rely on lower-level inputs from their bodies to inform those processes. Yet when we actually reach out our hand for that muffin (or, knowing we're headed to dinner soon, decide to skip it), it's our mind making the decision. How do minds actually control bodies, getting their bodies to do what their minds want them to? In other words, what is the source of our free will? To answer this question, we need to further unpack the grand hierarchy.

Atomic activity is unimaginably fast—millions of interactions happen every second, involving infinitesimal particles moving at the speed of light. Things get slower on the molecular level, as different elements combine and recombine. Cellular processes are even slower, relying on processes such as diffusion and transport across cell membranes within living systems. Organ processes—digestion, blood flow, and so on—are slower still. This general trend of slower functioning at higher levels of the grand hierarchy continues up through the brain—and, eventually, into the world, first in our relationships with others and then all the way to the top, where culture evolves and changes slowest of all.

This general trend is only what we would expect, given the assumption that each new level of organization is built upon the levels below it. The level below supplies the building blocks, but the level above evolved to organize those blocks, according to its own rules. Then, the next level up organizes the blocks that *it* is given, and so on up the chain. For example, cells organize trillions of different chemical substances; organ systems organize billions of different cells; minds organize millions of different neurons; and large corporations organize thousands of minds. Each higher level works more slowly than the levels below it. And each higher level appeared more recently in the long process of evolution.

And so we can see why reductionists are so tempted to look down in the hierarchy for explanations of behavior. According to reductionists, something more basic or elemental, something faster, explains something that is slower and more complex—such as cellular processes explaining organ processes, or brain processes explaining cognitive processes. At times, these kinds of explanations are indeed the right ones. In sickle cell anemia, for example, the failure of the circulatory system to deliver sufficient oxygen to other organ systems is reducible to a problem with an important constituent of the circulatory system—namely, its red blood cells, which are unable to carry much oxygen due to their sicklelike shape.

The sickle cell anemia example illustrates a very important fact: that, very often, reductionistic explanations apply best when a lower-level system is *failing* in its proper role. The blood cells are misshapen, preventing the circulation system from working correctly. Or the brain is damaged, preventing the person from thinking effectively. Or a player on a team is playing in a self-centered way, damaging the functioning of the multi-body team. In other words, lower-level, reductionistic explanations are usually most relevant when something goes wrong—otherwise, lower levels tend to hum along, supporting the activity above.

Let's consider brain injuries. In 1966, Charles Whitman stabbed his mother and his wife to death, then climbed to the top of a building at the University of Texas in Austin, where he shot and killed fourteen more people.[1] Whitman himself was then shot at the scene, and an autopsy was performed. It turned out he had a large tumor growing in his brain. Did the tumor make his actions uncontrollable, and excuse him from responsibility? According to the logic of the grand hierarchy, the answer to both questions is yes: the lower-level brain systems supporting Whitman's decision-making were compromised, such that he was not able to rationally consider and evaluate alternatives during the period he committed the murders—and was thus missing a key component of List's model of free will. Such people should be constrained and treated, not punished.

Some free-will skeptics would say that the chain of causes leading from Whitman's brain tumor to his terrible behavior was no different in principle from the chain of causes leading anybody's brain to do anything. But how do such skeptics get away with turning us all into brain-damaged beings? Blithely equating abnormal and normal functioning seems too extreme. Thus, some philosophers propose that free will and responsibility only apply when people have the brain systems they need to choose properly. In this view (which I agree with), the causation for behavior is only reducible to lower-level factors when lower-level systems fail. Otherwise, higher levels are typically in control and must be held responsible.

This point takes us to the flip side of the reductionist perspective: the holistic perspective.[2] Researchers and theorists taking a holistic perspective look up in the hierarchy for answers, seeking causal arrows that point down. Some higher-level situation contains or entrains the phenomenon to be explained, imposing its structure upon the lower-level process. For example, why are my neighbors and I staying home as I write these words in early 2021? Because our communities are fighting COVID-19. Why did Tony's body launch itself into the air at time t? Because, in his mind, he had just decided to take the shot. Why did a particular team win the league championship? Because of how well they played together as a team, becoming more than just the sum of the individual players and talents. These are all holistic (upward-looking, top-down) explanations.

Perhaps you saw the 2020 documentary series *The Last Dance*, about Michael Jordan and the Chicago Bulls, who dominated professional basketball in the 1990s. The documentary shows that the Bulls' success wasn't just because of Michael Jordan; the whole cast of the team enabled its success. Each player was assigned a distinct role and played it willingly and effectively, orchestrated by the coaching maestro Phil Jackson and the crafty general manager Jerry Krause. They created higher-level systems that "reached down" to holistically affect the operating conditions and success of the lower-level process (the team's play).

Reductionism has paid large dividends in science by illuminating the more basic processes that support and enable phenomena of interest. It is fair to say that reductionism has dominated science throughout history, and that it continues to dominate even today. But holism has also paid important dividends, helping to explain how larger-scale patterns can have top-down effects on the smaller-scale processes constituting them. Still, holistic theories are always threatened by reductionism because they are less parsimonious—they are not as simple, and insist on taking more factors, and more complex factors, into account. Do we really need to do that, asks the reductionist, or can those complex factors ultimately be reduced to more basic factors? Maybe the Bulls' success really was all due to Michael Jordan, so we don't have to think about team-level factors. Or maybe Tony's decision really was determined by microlevel brain processes, having nothing to do with his experience of making a decision.

One way of thinking about holistic (top-down) effects is via the concept of "emergence."[3] Emergent properties are properties manifested by a functional system that are not shown by any of the parts of the system taken alone; they only emerge when the system operates as a whole. Wetness is an emergent property of large collections of water molecules within a particular temperature range; behavior is an emergent property of living things, operating in their environment; cognition is an emergent property of human brains, modeling that environment; making choices is an emergent property of human personality, deciding what to do; and a team's excellent play is an emergent property of the separate players, all acting in concert. Continuing the theme, executive leadership is an emergent property of institution-level processes, and government is an emergent property of national-level processes.

Consider the CEO of a manufacturing corporation. She is a human being (with a personality) who has risen to a position of being able to control the corporation's decisions. In other words, by processes constructed by the "cells" of the corporation, that is, by individual employees operating in concert, this woman has emerged at the top of her company's organization, and now, she decides for that company.

Suppose the CEO exercises her functional autonomy and decides to shut down a manufacturing facility that is currently underperforming. This decision has a large impact, causing much disruption in the ranks of the corporation and a big increase in unemployment in the plant's town. Because she controls the operations of the company, she can influence the daily lives of thousands of people "down inside" the corporation, and all of the trillions of cells and kajillions of atoms contained within each person. Notice also the interdependence of the two levels of organization: without a corporation, there could be no CEO; but once a CEO emerges, she has a top-down (or holistic) impact upon the functioning of the corporation as well as upon all the people contained down within that corporation.

If the CEO's decision to shut down the plant is a bad one, her company may suffer. Maybe she will be fired as a result, by the very highest level of organization in the corporation, its board of directors. Still, while she was in the executive's office, she was the one making the choices for the company. She was free to screw up her company! Similarly, we are free to screw up our lives if we choose badly.

It's important to note, however, that any level of organization can influence behavior. Even the random decay of a proton at the atomic level might affect a person's behavior—perhaps causing a momentary nerve-firing to be amplified into a subliminally felt itch, resulting in the behavior of scratching. At the top end of the hierarchy, a cultural norm or expectation might influence a person inside that culture to make decisions (such as "Marry the man my parents tell me to marry," or "Circumcise our son").

Whether a particular level of the hierarchy has influence on a behavior depends in large part on the nature of the behavior. A trip to the snack cabinet might best be explained by a stomach hunger pang, at the organ systems level, or perhaps even lower, by low blood glucose in the muscle cells. But this isn't always the case—maybe the snacking is better explained by a person's momentary desire to escape boredom, a personality process taking place at a much higher level.

These distinctions may seem academic, but they have real implications for how we evaluate behavior and attempt to modify it. A person seeking psychiatric treatment is likely to be influenced by higher-level processes, such as dissatisfaction with life at the personality level, the urgings of a spouse at the social interactions level, or even the order of a court, at the societal level. In such cases, a psychiatrist may suggest talk therapy to help clients change the things causing them dissatisfaction (or perhaps change their perspective on those things). But perhaps the cause of someone's distress is really much further down in the hierarchy, having resulted from an imbalance of neurotransmitters. Here, all the psychiatrist needs to do to solve the problem is to prescribe the right medication. Of course, in most cases, multiple factors in the hierarchy are at play. You may head to the snack cabinet because you are a little bit hungry (on the level of organ systems) *and* a little bit bored (on the level of personality). You may feel depressed because you are unfulfilled in your job (at the level of organizational relationships) *and* because you have a genetic predisposition to developing clinical depression (at the level of cells).

Every person is unique, as is every situation. If we were able to collect enough data about what was happening up and down the hierarchy for each person, at each moment, and develop a sophisticated enough prediction model, then perhaps we could do a pretty good job predicting what people would do next. But we could never do a perfect job of predicting what they would do next.

How many levels down in the hierarchy do we need to go to have such a model? Generally speaking, this is an empirical question: let's collect the data, then find out which pieces matter most. But, as we saw in Chapter 1, with the example of Richard Dawkins's motorcar, we typically find that the further down we go, the less direct relevance there is to the phenomenon of interest. This is because the basic building blocks are so far away from the action. They're part of the background, not the foreground (again, unless they malfunction).

Let's go back to Tony's choice of whether to shoot at time *t*. As should be apparent by now, we probably don't need to enlist the help of particle physicists, or the help of chemists, to understand why Tony took the shot. It is possible we could get some traction by considering Tony's organic or neural processes, but probably not very much (again, unless there was something wrong with them). Instead, the sciences of cognitive, personality, and social psychology are best positioned to explain his behavior. Even neuroscientists, attempting to model cognition at the level of neurons, will need cognitive- and personality-type theories to know how to conceptualize and model the high-level processes that are organizing and controlling the neurons. Without the concept of a mental intention, microlevel neural processes make little sense, at least in terms of explaining macrolevel behaviors.

～⌒

In talking about the grand hierarchy, we've left out one of its most curious features. Within nonliving matter, compounds tend to break down into simpler compounds—a process called entropy. But living creatures do the opposite, maintaining themselves, until the moment of their deaths, at a high level of order. This is called negentropy. In negentropy, complexity is maintained or even increased. A functioning human body is a wildly improbable thing and would never appear randomly. It only works because each system in the body is able to do its part for the whole, from biochemistry up to cells up to organs up to nervous systems, brains, and personality processes. We are fabulously complex, and we manage to keep motoring along for seventy, eighty, even ninety or more years—fighting off the constant pull of disorder and death to remain alive another day. Indeed, the process of coping with challenges actually strengthens and improves the systems involved, as when a child's immune system, through exposure to novel pathogens, learns to better fight off illness. According to the Nobel Prize–winning chemist Ilya Prigogine, living systems "dissipate entropy": that is, they neutralize threats to their current organization by diversifying their functioning in response to those threats.[4] By adapting to challenges, they grow, becoming more complex than they were before.

So how do organisms cope and dissipate entropy in order to adapt and grow? And how do they exercise free will more generally? These are very complicated questions. But the simplest answer is: by controlling things.

The science of control theory and control systems is huge and sophisticated, ranging from computer science to engineering to medicine—as well as psychology. It is built on two surprisingly simple but powerful ideas: negative and positive feedback.

Generally speaking, negative feedback means that information is being used to reduce discrepancies between the system's standards and its current condition.[5] The system has the ability to detect a deflection from its set point or standard and then to initiate processes designed to eliminate the deflection, returning the system back to its steady state. All our body's systems use negative feedback in one way or another as they try to preserve homeostasis (or balance). For example, cell membranes maintain the chemical makeup of the interior of the cell within narrow limits by opening and closing ion channels. Glands regulate the levels of various hormones in the bloodstream. In technology, thermostats, cruise-control systems, and even missile guidance systems work along a similar logic: when the system starts to drift off course, it is brought back in line.

Negative feedback processes typically take the form of TOTE loops. TOTE, a term first proposed by George Miller and his colleagues in 1960, stands for "Test-operate-test-exit."[6] After the goal is set, a monitoring system "tests" for discrepancies. If a discrepancy is detected, a separate system "operates" to help fix the problem, then the monitoring system "tests" again. The recurring loop continues until there is no more discrepancy, after which the system "exits" the process.

TOTE loops run automatically throughout the body below the level of conscious awareness. The autonomic nervous system in our brain stems regulates conditions within (and between) our organ systems: the skin, the stomach, the blood, body temperature, and much else. Within each organ system, there are subprocesses occurring by which functioning is monitored and adjusted. Down at the level of microbiology, each individual cell is constantly taking actions to regulate and preserve its own state—there are TOTEs all the way down.

When it comes to our physiology, free will isn't a factor— the TOTE loops are automatic, running like machines. It's not even clear what "free will" could mean down at these low levels of the hierarchy. But minds (the systems that control the behavior of bodies) are not regulating physical parameters like enzymes, temperature, heart rate, and the like. Instead, they are manipulating information. The properties of information-processing systems go beyond the properties of the physical systems that constitute them.

To illustrate what I mean, consider the following true story. A moment ago I scratched my ear, prompted by a subtle itch. My nonconscious goal: remove the itch. The goal was met by the microlevel TOTE process of adjusting the scratching until it hit just the right spot (relief!). Soon after that, I formulated the goal, while writing, to "think of a concrete example of the universal TOTE point I am trying to make." Asking myself this question caused my nonconscious mind to seek possible answers, and it presented me with several possibilities, one of which was the itching and scratching episode. If you're reading about it now, I must have chosen to leave it in the book.

Here's the main point: thinking is a TOTE process in the same way that cellular regulation is a TOTE process. To think is to first set a goal or standard ("What was the name of that actress?"), then try to reduce the discrepancy between the goal ("Knowing the name") and the current state ("Not knowing the name"). In the scratching example, my intentional process directed my nonconscious mind to provide me with a set of alternatives to consider. It obliged me. I then picked one of the alternatives and continued writing.

TOTE processes at this level perfectly exemplify List's three-part definition of free will: an agent is able to consider alternatives, form intentions, and enact behavior. Were my actions caused by my neurons? The itch almost certainly was (including the nerves in my skin), and the involuntary scratching arguably was as well. But my decision to include the incident in the book was *my* choice, not my neurons' choice: I run my neurons (if they're working properly) at least as much as they run me.

Another interesting thing about my own mental TOTE process, in the scratching story, was that the goal or standard for that process, namely, "Find a good low-level example of my mind/body system executing a TOTE loop," was one that had never before appeared in my mind. It was a novel and likely one-time goal that arose in the process of my moment-to-moment direction of the mental activity in which I was embedded. This is the magic of our self-organizing mental systems: that they can be repurposed or reprogrammed on the fly as we ask ourselves questions we have never before asked. "What was the name of that book I picked up at the library last Thursday? Hmm...oh yes, Arthur Koestler's *The Ghost in the Machine*." "Why don't I like that TV show? Hmm...because the acting is wooden."

A skeptic might ask, "How can mental TOTE processes be said to have causal force, when we have no knowledge of the processes that constitute them?" After all, a mental intention is built on countless events occurring down in our atoms, cells, and brains, events of which we are totally ignorant.

My response is that this ignorance simply doesn't matter, as long as those processes aren't causing us to do things we would not agree with if we knew about them. And again, this only tends to happen when the lower-level systems are malfunctioning (as in Charles Whitman's tumor-driven shooting).

In short, human decision-makers don't have be omniscient, aware of every factor that influences their decisions; they just have to be able to make adjustments as they learn more about a situation. The same is true for CEOs, who are in charge of making decisions for their corporations. They don't know everything about the companies they direct, and they can't; there's simply too much information. But they can find out more as needed and fix the problems they discover.

Negative feedback—taking action to reduce discrepancies, or to maintain a stable state—is only half the story. Positive feedback is also important. It doesn't mean to give praise, as we think of it in our daily interactions with others, although there is a connection. With positive feedback, discrepancies are amplified rather than reduced, so that the system goes away from, not back to, its former state. Consider childbirth: it starts slowly but then speeds up through positive feedback. First, the child's head puts pressure on the cervix. Receptor cells in the cervix signal the brain, which causes the release of oxytocin in the blood. Back at the cervix, the oxytocin stimulates more frequent, larger contractions, causing further release of oxytocin, and so on. The status quo is left behind, so that the child may be born. Notice that both bottom-up and top-down processes are involved here: the cervix has bottom-up influence on the brain that regulates it, which then has top-down influence on the cervix, which has further effects on the brain, and so on.

How do positive feedback loops operate at the levels of personality and cognition? Here, praise can play a role: the student or child makes a new mental connection, and the teacher or parent's praise can help reward, and consolidate, that step forward. Creative processes provide another great example of positive feedback in action. An artist (or scientist) is looking for a new idea and detects a glimmer of possibility in a particular insight or approach. She then works with that insight, trying to push it further to explore its still unseen implications. She is trying to ride a wave toward something as far from her own status quo as possible. In the process she might be battling negative feedback standards (play it safe, don't take a risk, go back where you started). But if she is courageous, she might be able to give birth to a brand-new scientific idea or artistic product, even one that becomes much used or admired by others.

Here's another example of positive feedback: my writing this book! At first, I was reluctant to begin, because the concept of free will is so confusing and difficult, and because so many people had already written about it. One morning, early in the pandemic, I wrote a first paragraph, and I thought it was okay—I was encouraged enough to keep going. Over time, I became more encouraged. A year and a half later, I had basically finished what you hold in your hands—a brand-new intellectual product that no scientific theory could have predicted, certainly not to the level of chapters and individual sentences. Yes, my dad might have predicted that I'd eventually write a book about free will. But there's no way that he (or anyone) could have predicted this exact sentence!

The concepts of positive feedback and dissipative systems create the possibility of a profound evolutionary ethos for understanding "optimal functioning" or "self-actualization." This ethos, or basic guiding principle, would say that we are at our best when we maximally dissipate entropy—using threats and stressors as prompts and inspirations to develop ever more complex and creative ways of functioning. Also, we live best when we are able to "ride the positive feedback train" to create new complexity, not just in ourselves, but also in the larger systems in which we are embedded. A great artist, author, or inventor is one whose accomplishments resonate far beyond his or her own life up into the broader cultural sphere. John Prine, the late folk musician, for example, turned his angst into songs. In so doing, he was able to contribute to the larger world in ways that touched all who knew him and his music.

We can apply this ethos not just to individuals but also to entire societies. Does a society give rise to maximal humanity, culture, innovation, and progress? I would argue that the main determinant is how well the society treats its most precious resource: the human potential of each of its members. In an ideal society, no human potential would be wasted; every person would be helped to develop to the maximum extent, so that society would gain the potential innovations coming from everyone (and it can't be known in advance which people will contribute the most). Unfortunately, in current world societies huge amounts of human potential are squandered. Too many children don't get what they need to maximally develop. What if we didn't throw away so many lives?

So where, in the grand hierarchy, is the thing that we call "us"? Where is the self? The answer is that it's at the personality level of organization. Selves exist in a mental world of stories and narratives, and are ignorant of what is happening down in their own brain machinery. Selves are responsible for making and endorsing choices for the body. In the process, they regulate and control their own bodies more or less effectively (do we get enough sleep, do we exercise, do we find worthwhile activities to do?).

Selves also exist in a world of other selves, and they operate in that social world, more or less effectively, via their choices and decisions. As the grand hierarchy shows, we can be strongly influenced by other people. But still, it is always "up to us" to decide what to say and do next, and to understand what went wrong when our choices don't work out well. The case of Tony again provides a great example: As he chooses whether to shoot, the context of his relationship with his coach and teammates certainly might influence his choice. But he was also free to ignore that social context, and to ignore what he thought his coach would have had him do.

*   *   *

It's critical to understand that the momentary conscious self stands at the "crux-point" of human reality, between all the biology below, and all the sociology above. We're literally making it up as we go along! It makes sense that we'd find the main organizing principle of human reality at the personality level of the grand hierarchy, given that this level evolved to control the complex biocomputer that each of us was born with. Our behaviors are strongly affected by the decisions that we selves make, the intentions we form. Not all of our intentions are conscious: often we do things involuntarily or automatically, without reflection. But the self operates primarily at the level of conscious, verbalizable intentions of the form "I think I'll do X." If we're paying attention, making good-faith efforts, and trying to learn from our mistakes, then our inalienable choosing capacity gives us the power to live rich and fulfilling lives. We will now start delving into personality psychology to better understand how this works.

CHAPTER 4

IF WE'RE FREE, WHY DON'T WE FEEL FREE?

I hope I've begun to convince you that our feeling of actively living our lives—of making choices day to day and even moment to moment—isn't necessarily a delusion. In truth, I've never seen a good argument for why evolution would have given humans the metabolically expensive ability to imagine that we are mental agents in charge—the ability to create, live inside of, and partially direct such a complex inner movie—if we weren't actually in charge, at least in some important ways. It would be such a big waste of energy and processing space if there were no return on the investment. Evolution doesn't usually work that way.

But if we are always free to choose, then an important question arises: *Why do we feel so controlled sometimes?* Why do we spend so much time doing things we don't want to do, and so little time doing things we do want to do? And why do we sometimes feel so pushed around by life, by circumstances, and even by the people we love?

With this question, we have arrived at the research domain of self-determination theory (SDT), the world's most comprehensive and best-supported theory of human motivation. SDT has been under development for more than fifty years and is still going strong (several hundred researchers from around the world will attend the next international SDT conference, in 2023). SDT is a big theory, and I don't want to burden you with all of the details of its six "mini-theories," although we'll touch on five of them before the book is done. My goal in this chapter is simply to give an overview of the main ways that SDT thinks about human autonomy and to explain some of the studies that have led to these conclusions. I'll also explain why the feeling of being autonomous and self-determined is so important for our health, effectiveness, and well-being, even if the feeling is "just an illusion," as determinists insist.

SDT began in the late 1960s and early 1970s with the pioneering research of Ed Deci.[1] Deci was a long-haired graduate student working in industrial-organizational (IO) psychology. A basic assumption of IO psychology is that people work for pay. Thus, being paid to do X should always be more motivating than not being paid, and the more people are paid for doing X, the greater their motivation should be. This is simply operant behaviorism, of the B. F. Skinner variety: the idea that animals (including people) repeat behaviors for which they are positively reinforced, or for which they receive larger amounts of positive reinforcement. If we receive desirable rewards (such as money) from the environment after doing a particular action, says behaviorism, then we should become mechanically conditioned to do the action again, via a stimulus-response connection.

Deci had some doubts about this idea. What if he could instead show that people were *less* motivated the more money they received as a reward? What if money, in some circumstances, actually functioned like a punishment instead of like a reward? By definition, a punishment is any stimulus that reduces the likelihood that the preceding behavior will be repeated. Suppose you smile at someone, and that person frowns back. If you don't smile at that individual anymore, then the frown (the stimulus) is said to have punished your smiling behavior, reducing its likelihood of recurring. Usually, a punishment (like the frown) feels unpleasant, which is why people try to avoid repeating behaviors that brought punishment. Wouldn't it be ironic if money functioned as a punishment for some kinds of behavior?

Deci decided to put his hypothesis to the test and devised an ingenious and subversive set of experiments. He chose to use a type of puzzle that was all the rage at that time, the Soma puzzle. The Soma puzzle consists of seven colorful and irregularly shaped pieces that can fit together to form a cube. Mathematically, it's a simpler version of the Rubik's cube, which came later. The Rubik's cube, however, twists and turns, and the challenge has to do with arranging the colors, whereas the Soma cube's seven pieces come apart entirely, and the challenge is to put them back together—and not always into a cube. Particular Soma puzzles involve trying to assemble the seven unique pieces into various larger shapes after seeing pictures of those shapes. People naturally enjoyed playing with Soma cubes; it enjoyed great popularity at the time. Deci wondered if he could kill that enjoyment.

Deci randomly assigned each of his study participants to one of two conditions. In the first (neutral control) condition, participants were simply asked to spend a few minutes "trying out some of the puzzles, to see if you like them." After five minutes the experimenter excused himself, supposedly to make copies of a final survey, telling individual participants that while they waited, they could either do some more Soma puzzles or look at some magazines (today, participants would just take out their cell phones!). Many of these participants kept playing with the puzzles during this "free-choice" period. Deci timed them, unbeknownst to them, through a one-way window. And why shouldn't they want to keep going, rather than read a boring magazine? Deci chose the game because of its addictive properties.

In the second experimental condition, participants were instead told at the beginning that they would receive one dollar for each Soma puzzle they correctly solved, for up to five puzzles. This was the only difference between the two conditions: the second group of participants knew they could earn money by solving the puzzles.

And during the free-choice period in this second condition, what happened was exactly what Deci had predicted: participants who knew they could earn money by doing the puzzles spent less time, on average, doing additional puzzles than the participants who had not been told they could earn money, and more time thumbing through magazines. They had been "punished by rewards," as the writer Alfie Kohn later put it.[2] When the time came for them to exercise free choice, they chose not to play anymore.

In interpreting his findings, Deci embraced a radical new idea that was emerging in the 1960s: that behavior can be *intrinsically motivated*. This means that doing a behavior can be its own reward—it is fun and interesting, and people don't have to be reinforced by external rewards and tokens to do it. Intrinsically motivated behaviors are the things that we choose to do when we get to do what we want: relaxing on the weekend, going on vacation, celebrating Mardi Gras. Today, the concept of intrinsic motivation is almost universally accepted, and it is easily seen even in nonhuman animals (just search for "curious cats" on YouTube). The bigger the brain, the more intrinsic motivation it has—the more it "plays."

But in the 1960s, intrinsic motivation was a radical idea. Psychologists through the 1950s and into the 1960s (before the so-called cognitive revolution) were not comfortable with the idea that people "moved themselves" or "directed themselves." Research psychology hadn't come very far up the grand hierarchy—it hadn't even reached the cognitive level yet. Researchers were much more reductionist in their explanations, and more reluctant to accept "mentalistic" explanations. As reductionists, they often saw subjective experiences as mere epiphenomena. Thus they thought subjective experiences could never be *causes* of future events; they were only *effects* of past events, just dead ends in the chain.

The real causes of our behavior, according to the drive and behaviorist theories of the 1940s and 1950s, had to be some combination of physical factors (one's biological drives) and historical factors (one's conditioning).[3] These were brought together under the formula "Motivation$_x$ = Drive × Habit$_x$." This formula says that we are only motivated by the need to reduce our biological drives, such as for air or food, which naturally build up over time. And we are motivated to do this mainly in ways that have worked in the past—that is, for which we've acquired a conditioned "habit." A hungry undergraduate keeps returning to a particular snack machine for food, and a swimmer keeps returning to the surface for air. The problem that Deci's experiment helped illustrate was that the drive theory formula couldn't explain most of what people do, such as going to movies, or to classes, or taking walks or bike rides, or having conversations with other people—despite a lot of attempted modifications to the formula to try to account for them. As a result, drive theory was ultimately abandoned.

Today, we know that intrinsic motivation is a real thing and that it is really important. Self-directed exploration and play are primary factors in human learning and development. Our curiosity, more than anything else, is what promotes deep and lasting learning, not the grades or the praise we receive. As children, our brains remain empty until we, their operators, get interested and engaged in the world (grasp the finger, shake the rattle, learn to walk, talk to people). A subjective agent (that is, each of us) has to want to put brain capacities to use in order to develop those capacities. In this sense, intrinsic motivation is the tangible expression of the basic organizational impulse within the human mind, which includes our inherent desire to explore our worlds. With intrinsic motivation, we can do almost anything. Without it, we may be mere drones—like pigeons pecking on keys to get their food, as in the behaviorist studies of the 1940s and 1950s.

Deci's greatest contribution was showing that intrinsic motivation is *fragile*. That is, intrinsic motivation is susceptible to "undermining." If powerful others start using rewards to shape our behavior, trying to get us to do what they want, we notice: it feels disagreeable, and it may even cause us to lose interest in doing what used to be a lot of fun. In other words, if we "cognitively evaluate" the situation and judge that the reward is meant to coerce us, then we may lose our intrinsic motivation. This, then, is the first of SDT's mini-theories: *cognitive evaluation theory.*

Consider a boy who loves to experiment with the family piano. He even teaches himself to play a song or two by ear. Then he is put on a regimen of lessons, with an agenda and a reinforcement schedule set by his parents. Regular practice times are scheduled and monitored to make sure the money spent on the lessons is worth it. The child's allowance is tied to his practicing. The end result, in too many cases, is that the child digs in his heels and permanently loses interest in music.

This kind of undermining can persist even over many years. In 2019, Arlen Moller and I published a study in which we surveyed 348 former varsity athletes from the University of Missouri, up to forty years after they graduated.[4] Our question was whether they still participated in their sport, or at least still followed the sport and cared about it. We compared two groups of former athletes: those who were on athletic scholarships during their varsity days (meaning their education and living expenses had been paid for), and those who were not on scholarships—so-called walk-ons.

It seemed safe to assume that the scholarship athletes were more serious about their sport and better at it back when they were in college. Logically, they should still be more interested in it today. But guided by Deci's early findings with the Soma puzzle, we hypothesized the opposite: that those who went to school on athletic scholarships would have less present-day intrinsic motivation (measured in terms of felt enjoyment, interest, and involvement in their sport) than the walk-ons. For the scholarship athletes, awareness of their paid status might permanently affect their experience of the sport.

And that is exactly what we found: the former scholarship athletes reported significantly less present-day intrinsic motivation for their sport than the former walk-ons—less interest in playing the sport or even watching it. The experience of playing for external rewards seemed to have undermined their intrinsic motivation for their sport even decades later.

A few years earlier, an undergraduate honors student, Mark White, and I found something similar in a study of professional athletes. We pulled together many years of US National Basketball Association and Major League Baseball data seeking evidence for the "contract year effect."[5] This is the idea that professional athletes perform better than average during seasons immediately before their contracts will be renegotiated. In those seasons, supposedly, they are extra motivated, because if they play well, they are more likely to get a big pay boost. But after the new contract is signed, their performance supposedly returns to the prior level. They don't play as well in the future as they did in the contract year. This idea was often talked about by the sports pundits but had been little tested with data.

Mark and I asked: What if athletes didn't just regress to their prior baselines after the contract year, but actually did *worse* than their first-year baseline, because their intrinsic motivation had been undermined by the intense money-focus of the contract year? What if the contract-year experience, in which they were constantly thinking about money, permanently dampened their enthusiasm for the sport?

The data we pulled together involved three-year sequences of statistics from professional basketball and baseball over the previous twenty years. These sequences covered the year before a player's contract year (the baseline), the contract year itself, and the year after the contract year (after the new contract took effect). We looked at both offensive statistics (points per game and shooting percentages for basketball, batting averages and home runs for baseball) and defensive statistics (shots blocked and steals for basketball, fielding range and put-outs for baseball).

In both the basketball and baseball samples, players' offensive statistics increased in the contract year compared to the year before. They were trying harder in response to the extrinsic incentive, trying to generate gaudy statistics, and it worked. The contract year boost was real. Still, players didn't do better in their defensive play during their contract years, presumably because fans and team officials don't pay as much attention to these statistics, or don't weight them as highly. Defensive play involves grinding it out, not being a star.

The most interesting finding of our study was exactly what we had predicted: after players had landed a new contract, during the third year of the sequence, their performance suffered in many ways—both their offensive and defensive performance. Players didn't just regress back to their previous baselines—that is, their level of performance in the first year of the sequence. Instead, they performed significantly *below* their initial baselines in the third year of the sequence. It seemed that athletes' strong rewards focus during the contract year had undermined their zest for the sport after the reward was obtained.

Note that we didn't measure athletes' intrinsic motivation directly—that would have been impossible. Instead, we inferred their motivation from their performance, under the assumption that intrinsic motivation usually produces better performance. Some have suggested another explanation for our finding: that players simply may not have worked out as hard before the third year, after they landed the big contract. Maybe they took it easy in their off-season training, and this was why they played worse in year three. But this explanation is still consistent with the conclusion that thoughts of money reduced their intrinsic motivation. Perhaps, after the contract year, working out in the off-season had become something the athletes did "only to get paid," rather than being a way to improve and excel at the game they once loved.

Early SDT thinking and research was rooted in the attempt to explain this effect. After a decade of research, Deci (and his student-turned-collaborator Richard Ryan) concluded that human beings have evolved a basic *need for autonomy*—a need to feel that they are doing things because they want to (or because they decide to), not because they have to (or are forced to). With very few exceptions (such as when they're making excuses), people need to experience themselves as the causal source and origin of their own behavior rather than feeling controlled and determined by external forces. When people feel autonomous, they tend to behave better than when they feel controlled. They are also more willing to take responsibility for their actions—to accept blame and reprimands as necessary. They're invested in what they're doing and want to do it right. They even tend to care more about others, not less, as you might think. It turns out that autonomy (owning one's behaviors) is psychologically different from independence (not caring what others want), even though they are frequently confused.

Many years of SDT research extended the original findings about how external rewards can undermine intrinsic motivation, showing that it holds true for many kinds of activities. It's not just puzzle-playing, or sports, that can be ruined. And the effect can extend to many other things besides money or grades, including deadlines, surveillance, competition, and even verbal rewards and praise. The common element among all these factors is that they can feel controlling. They can all be "cognitively evaluated" as coercive. They threaten to deprive people of their sense of autonomy, which wrecks their enjoyment of whatever activity is at hand.

Why is felt autonomy so important? This question leads us to the first of SDT's two most basic assumptions: that human beings are naturally curious, with an inborn propensity to explore the world and taste its offerings. They accomplish this through self-directed learning, making choices that both express and develop their growing minds. Via such intrinsic motivation they learn to run their own cognitive machinery while learning about the world. SDT is an organismic and living-systems theory: it emphasizes the creative and self-constructive nature of "human being"—where "being" is viewed as a verb, not just a noun. We are like a flame that burns—and like every flame, we can burn more or less brightly depending on the fuel at hand.

SDT's second basic assumption is that innate growth propensities may or may not be fueled by a person's social environment (family, school, relationships, and so on). To have a need—such as the human need to be an autonomous agent—is to be somewhat vulnerable: if that need isn't supported, or, even worse, if it is actively thwarted, then people may suffer. In such cases they tend to regress and can act in maladaptive or self-defeating ways.

In short, mental health and psychological growth depend on supportive conditions. A plant, in a way, is similar: to grow, it needs the right amount of light, the right soil, and a certain amount of water. In the wrong social conditions, people can wither just as plants can wither in the wrong environment. The plant analogy conveys an important principle: psychology is ultimately a biological science; it just happens to focus on mental activity rather than biological activity. Biological and mental activity are both living processes, and both may either function well (the person grows and thrives) or not (the person languishes and withers).

SDT pays a lot of attention to the interface between the *personality* level of the grand hierarchy (how we run our own bodies) and the *social relations* level (how we interact with other bodies). This is the important "phase transition" where the one meets the many, where the singular person becomes part of the plurality of people, where each of our own personal systems is tested by having to mesh with larger social systems. Social psychology is the science that addresses this particular level of organization by studying how different personalities interact with and influence each other. The intrinsic motivation undermining effect that Deci discovered is considered to be a classic social psychology finding.

SDT focused its attention early on upon a very important type of social relationship—the kind in which there is unequal power. In such relationships, one person (the top dog) is in a position of authority over a second person (the underdog), with higher status and more power, including the power to make the second person's life difficult for not complying with the first person's dictates. We all find ourselves in unequal power relations in life: as children, students, employees, patients, and team members. That is, we encounter parents, teachers, employers, doctors, and coaches who have the social leverage to boss us around, should they choose. Often, they do choose to do just that, or worse. A coach might make his players begin a rigid and unpleasant training regimen. Another coach might order a player to hurt a player on another team. Yet another coach might even coerce his players into performing sexual favors. You can probably think of your own examples of authorities in your life who tried to control and manipulate you, using their social power as leverage. In too many cases, authorities function as despots who demoralize and demotivate the people in their charge by denying them choice. They abuse their authority and undermine our faith in the higher level of social organization they represent.

Ideally (and sometimes in actuality), authorities function as wise mentors: they understand the needs of their subordinates and help them act in ways that benefit both the subordinates themselves and others. Many of us can remember that special teacher, coach, or parent who taught us how to trust, how to regulate ourselves, and how to treat other people. Learning how to use social power wisely is one of the most difficult skills in the human repertoire, and a skill that becomes more important the older we get. It involves the ability to operate the controls of the social world in such a way that all parties benefit from the process. In some ways healthy social skills are like healthy organs: if our kidneys work well, then our cells (below the kidneys) and our brains (above them) thrive—and if our relationships work well, then our personalities (below) and social groups (above) thrive.

Hundreds of SDT studies now show that receiving autonomy support from the authorities above us—being encouraged by them to make our own choices—is critical for our development and sense of well-being.[6] Autonomy-supportive authorities listen to those under them, care about them, relate to them, explain things to them, and allow them as much leeway as they can, given the situation. They try to minimize or deemphasize the power differential between themselves and those under them ("Yeah, I'm your boss, but really we're just people"). When authorities can do this, things go better for both parties (a win-win situation). By treating their subordinates respectfully, autonomy-supportive authorities get more cooperation from those subordinates and better results. They are stoking their charges' intrinsic motivation, helping them to do the best they can.

Autonomy support may be especially important in high-pressure situations. Undergraduate honors student Anna Watson and I published another study about athletes in 2011.[7] We looked at several hundred undergraduates involved in sports: recreational participants (those playing on intramural sports teams, such as basketball or volleyball, against other student teams); club participants (those playing on a university-sponsored team, such as soccer, that travels and plays other universities' teams, but without receiving scholarships or major institutional support); and varsity participants (those playing on a major university team, such as football or basketball, who receive scholarships and are coached by professional staff). Each team had a coach, and we measured each coach's autonomy support by asking all athletes to rate their agreement with six statements according to a standard scale. These included, for example, "My coach tries to understand how I see things," "My coach provides me with choices and options," and "My coach listens to how I would like to do things." We averaged the responses and then examined the correlations between perceived autonomy support from the coach and the players' intrinsic motivations for playing as well as their overall evaluation of the sports experience.

What we found was that at all three levels of sports participation, autonomy support mattered—nobody likes a controlling coach. But autonomy-supportive coaching mattered most at the varsity level, and it had the biggest effects there. Varsity athletes are engaged in high-pressure activities that are often big revenue generators for the university. Under those circumstances, it makes a big difference whether the athletes feel the coach is on their side, rather than feeling that the coach is exploiting and controlling them for the coach's own benefit. In fact, having an autonomy-supportive coach buffered varsity athletes from the pressures they could feel from fans, reporters, and alumni, whereas having a controlling coach made those pressures worse.

It can be difficult for big-time coaches to relinquish some control and allow athletes to regulate themselves; the stakes are high, and coaches need to win for their own reasons—a consistently losing coach won't be employed for much longer. But the benefits of being autonomy supportive are clear. If coaches can manage to become wise mentors rather than drill sergeants, they will get the most from their athletes. The athletes will be able to retain their intrinsic motivation, which enables them to play better and more creatively. Importantly, this doesn't mean coaches *shouldn't* impose structure, have expectations, offer rewards, or even impose punishments: it just means they should do these things in a sensitive way, with good humor, keeping in mind how they would feel if the roles were reversed.

We've been talking about intrinsic motivation, in which we do something for fun. Of course, not everything we do can be interesting and enjoyable. What about cleaning the house, changing diapers, or finishing a quarterly report—are we supposed to have intrinsic motivation for doing these kinds of tasks?

This is a very good question, and in the late 1980s SDT began to address it. SDT's second mini-theory, *organismic integration theory*, states that a person can willingly perform a behavior they don't like if they have managed to internalize it into their sense of self. Internalizing a behavior means that we come to see the value, meaning, and importance of that behavior. We fully assent to it, even if we don't enjoy doing it. Cleaning the house becomes much more agreeable (if not yet fun) when we have come to agree that it is important, perhaps because we enjoy spending time in a clean home. Such behaviors express our desire to be a certain kind of person living in a certain way, and thus we can do them cheerfully.

This second type of autonomous motivation is called *identified motivation*, and it expresses our mature commitments and agreements. Identified motivation reflects our capacity for free will in an important new way, because it helps us get ourselves to do things we don't like doing. No other animal can do this—it takes the frontal lobe capacities that are only available to the operators of human brains. But it also takes a subjective agent who can make a decision to use those capacities.

In 2019 I published a study of Pacific Crest Trail (PCT) through-hikers that aimed to explain how people persevere through tasks that are challenging or even unpleasant.[8] PCT through-hikers are attempting to complete the entirety of a 2,650-mile-long trail stretching from Mexico to Canada through mountainous terrain. Some people do the trail in parts over the course of many years. But the through-hikers I studied were trying to do it within a single spring and summer. (You may have heard of the PCT from the book *Wild* by Cheryl Strayed, or the movie based on it, which starred Reese Witherspoon.) The route is grueling. It goes over steep passes and snowfields (often at

12,000 or 13,000 feet), across raging creeks, and through water-less deserts. It requires resupplying oneself along the way, often by hiking miles down from the mountains into nearby towns and then hiking back up. To complete the trail in just one season requires walking an average of nearly 20 miles every day, typically with more than 50 pounds on your back.

In the spring of 2018 I was able to recruit ninety-five aspiring PCT through-hikers for my study—as a backpacker myself, I was able to get access to the relevant Facebook groups. In the first survey, before the hike started, I measured hikers' initial happiness levels as well as their intrinsic motivation for starting the hike. For the latter, I asked them to rate their agreement (or disagreement) with statements such as, "I will hike the PCT because it will be a pleasure," or ". . . because it will be challenging," or ". . . because it will be interesting." I also measured their identified motivation, using statements such as "I will hike the PCT because it will be meaningful to me," or ". . . because it is personally important to me," or ". . . because I see the value in it."

After their journey was over, in the fall of 2018, I had the hikers fill out a second survey in which they looked back on their experiences. This survey measured the same motivations, this time asking: "Near the end of your hike, why were you continuing on?" The fall survey also measured hikers' ending happiness levels and asked them whether they had actually completed the hike (about half of them had made it all the way to Canada). This study design allowed me to look at changes in hikers' motivations over time to see how the changes affected their ability to complete the trail. It also allowed me to examine hikers' happiness levels at the end compared to how they had felt at the beginning.

The pattern of results was highly unusual, but it made great sense from the perspective of identified motivation as applied to extreme sports. First, hikers' intrinsic motivation had plummeted by the end of the summer. What had started out as an exciting challenge became much more of a grim slog as the discomforts and difficulties mounted. In the language of SDT, there was a clear undermining effect. Hikers' intrinsic motivation and enjoyment was much reduced by the many inescapable problems along the way. But at the same time, their happiness levels went up, and it went up quite a lot, on average, from the beginning to the end of the hike—even if they didn't finish the entire 2,650-mile route.

Clearly, these hikers had done something very meaningful, something that gave them a significant sense of pride and purpose despite all the suffering. SDT's concept of identified motivation is the perfect term for it, and the data from the hikers confirmed it. But one finding was unusual: for many of the hikers, identified motivation increased over the course of the summer at the same time that intrinsic motivation was decreasing. Typically, the two forms of autonomous motivation track together—as identified motivation rises, intrinsic motivation rises along with it. This study allowed me to see what happens when they do not run in parallel. And what I found was that the most persistent PCT hikers had fully internalized their goal to complete the trail. They made it part of themselves, part of their identity, and that kept them going through the pain and difficulties.

My study also considered a third form of internal motivation, known as *introjected motivation*, which is based in guilt and self-pressure. The problem with introjection is that it is only partially internalized, like a bite of food that is only half-swallowed. It is as if one part of the person were forcing another part to complete the task. My participants rated themselves on this type of motivation by answering questions such as, "I want to hike the PCT because I'll feel bad about myself if I don't," or ". . . because I'd feel ashamed if I failed." Most people can think of examples of introjected motivation in their own lives—say, when you change the baby's diaper only because it's your turn, and you don't want to feel like a bad husband and father; or when you get yourself out the door for a morning run only by imagining how bad you'll feel about yourself if you don't. With introjected motivation, we are ambivalent—both wanting, and not wanting, to do something.

My PCT data showed that introjected motivation also increased in the hiker sample, even more than identified motivation did. Compared to their motivations at the beginning of the hike, the through-hikers became much more self-controlling over time, with many of them turning into harsh internal taskmasters. This isn't necessarily a good thing, because much research shows that introjected motivation tends to be associated with a lower sense of well-being. It is hard to feel guilty and happy at the same time.

How did the observed changes in internalized motivation over the summer affect participants' ability to finish the hike, and their happiness levels after the hike? Again, the results were fascinating, and right in line with SDT. Increases in both identified and introjected motivation were associated with greater distance covered on the trail as well as with actually finishing the hike. Participants who were able to build either of these two internalized forms of motivation, after their intrinsic motivation fell away, were better able to carry on. So, yes, introjected motivation can be valuable for getting ourselves to do things.

But again, introjected motivation doesn't feel fully autonomous, because we feel like we are forcing ourselves. The activity isn't fully satisfying. Consistent with this idea, I found that actually completing the PCT didn't further boost participants' post-hike sense of well-being *unless* they had also developed greater identified motivation over the summer. In other words, actually finishing the PCT only raised the hiker's sense of well-being if the hiker was fully identified with the journey. Completing the PCT *didn't* raise a hiker's sense of well-being if completion of the trail was driven by an increase in introjected motivation. Although guilt-based motivation helped them get the task done, it also took away much of the satisfaction and fulfillment they might otherwise have gotten from doing the trail.[9]

The main moral of the PCT study: we are best off if we can fully internalize our own behaviors, so that we wholeheartedly agree with and endorse what we do, even if the behaviors themselves are difficult or painful. With full internalization, we have fully accepted our own choices and have taken responsibility for them—just as is recommended by the existential perspective, which says we are always free and always responsible for what we do, whether we (currently) realize it or not. When we feel that we are forcing or guilting ourselves into doing something, it may be a sign that we should think more about what we're doing. Perhaps we can finish internalizing the behavior and then fully endorse it. Or maybe we should abandon the behavior altogether and find something more suitable to do. (We'll consider this important dilemma in much more detail in Chapter 7.)

How can we come to feel more self-determined in our behavior? My colleagues and I performed an interesting series of studies considering the role that mere aging plays in this process.[10] We hypothesized that as people get older they naturally tend to develop more internalized motivation for what they do, becoming more the felt authors of their own actions. In other words, on average, older people should learn (through experience) what they want and agree with, and should develop a stronger ability to resist social pressures that might push them to do things they disagree with. To test this hypothesis, we considered three behaviors that, almost by definition, are unlikely to be intrinsically motivated: paying taxes, voting in elections, and tipping servicepeople. These are "social duties" that many of us do only because we have to or are supposed to. The question: Do age and experience teach us to do these duties more willingly, with a sense of fully identifying with their importance?

That is exactly what we found in a study of participants ranging in age from seventeen to eighty-six. The older the participant, the more identified motivation they had for voting, tipping, and tax-paying. This was shown by a significant positive correlation between a participant's age and their level of identified motivation across the three duties. Older participants tended to see the duties as more meaningful and important, whereas younger participants had more introjected motivations—they had to force and guilt themselves into performing the duties. It seems that the aging process teaches people to fully endorse the things they are "supposed" to do, rather than doing them with internal reservations.

We found the same basic age difference in a study comparing college students (in their early twenties) to their own parents (in their forties or fifties).[11] College students filled out a survey in which they listed some of their own life-goals and rated their motivations for pursuing them. They gave us their parents' contact information, and our research team sent the same survey to the parents. We found that the parents had more identified (self-endorsed) motivation to pursue their own life-goals, whatever those goals were, than their children; in contrast, their children had more introjected (guilt-based) motivation for their life-goals. Once again, it seemed that people tend to mature over time, becoming more the felt authors of, and autonomous agents within, their own lives.[12]

We don't keep getting better forever, though. Aging imposes limits, and aging brains become more limited as well, both in terms of what they can remember and in terms of how well they can cope with novelty. Toward the very end of life, a person's sense of autonomy tends to decrease, as you might expect. Still, this usually doesn't happen until near death. Until then, maturational processes, toward increasing autonomy and felt free will, tend to hold sway.

෴

What specific situations help people internalize doing unpleasant behaviors, thereby developing more mature identified motivations? For the PCT through-hikers, it happened
in reaction to the enormous difficulties of the task they had
set themselves. For the older people performing social duties,
it happened gradually, through a process of maturation. But
what kinds of social contexts help people internalize their actions in the short term?

What helps the most is autonomy support from the authorities in the situation. When our teachers, employers, and
parents listen to us, when they respect our sense of self, and
when they clearly explain why they insist we do something,
then we are more likely to internalize doing that something,
no matter how tedious or boring it is. We willingly complete
the quarterly report, clean the house, or do the unpleasant exercises. If authorities instead use their power to try to force us
to do things, and to do them only their way, then we are im-
peded in our ability to connect those behaviors to our sense of
self.

A study I conducted with PhD student Neetu Abad (who
is now a behavioral scientist at the Centers for Disease Control and Prevention studying vaccine hesitancy) offers another
interesting example of how autonomy support influences the
process of internalizing motivation.[13] Our question in this
case was about what psychological processes allowed second-
generation immigrants (such as Neetu herself) to become bicultural. Second-generation immigrants are the children of
first-generation immigrants—their parents came to the new

country and culture, bringing their old culture and customs with them. The children in our study were either small at the time of the move or were born soon afterward.

Most first-generation immigrants would like their children to appreciate and accept the old culture, but they would also like their children to successfully adapt to the new culture. They want their children to feel connected to both cultures. But not all such parents are effective in instilling these values. In our study, we measured parental autonomy support by asking the children to complete the same scale used in the student athlete study described earlier—this time, with statements such as, "My parents try to understand how I see things," "My parents provide me with choices and options," and "My parents listen to how I would like to do things." We found that the more parents supported the autonomy of their children, allowing them to make their own decisions about their cultural identities, the more their children accepted and cherished the old ways as well as the new—the more bicultural they were (as measured by several standard scales). Giving children the freedom to question the old ways apparently caused them to accept those ways. But forcing a child to participate in a cultural practice, such as going to religious services, or taking language classes, can limit how much the child wants to continue the practice as an adult.

In other words, you can't *make* somebody genuinely believe that something is important. For the first-generation parents who tried it, forcing their children to accept the native culture backfired. It seems that all authorities can do is provide a context for subordinates to make their own decisions, trusting that they are more likely to understand, respect, and accept the authority's preferences if the authority supports the subordinate's own choice process. In the immortal words of Richard Bach, in his book *Jonathan Livingston Seagull*: "If you love someone, set them free. If they come back, they're yours; if they don't they never were."

So far, we've been talking about intrinsic motivation, identified motivation, and the importance of receiving autonomy support from authorities for both types of autonomous motivation. We've touched on two SDT mini-theories: cognitive evaluation theory (how people evaluate the intentions behind proffered rewards, perhaps losing their intrinsic motivations), and organismic integration theory (how people can internalize unenjoyable behaviors). Now let's talk about another way that SDT sheds light on the issue of psychological autonomy, with its crucial relevance for health and development. SDT's third mini-theory, *causality orientations theory*, focuses on three free-will-relevant personality styles or traits.[14]

What are these three orientations? In the first, *autonomy orientation*, people pay attention to aspects of the environment that stimulate their intrinsic motivation, that support choice, and that provide informational feedback (so they can learn how to improve). For example, when offered a new job, they say to themselves, "I wonder if the work will be interesting." Autonomously oriented people are looking for situations and activities in which they can be self-directed, and in which they can learn about and develop their own capacities.

They tend to take more responsibility for their behavior, and to support the autonomy of others just as much as they support their own. It is as if they are operating as agents with free will, who want others to be free as well. Autonomy orientation is correlated with many positive characteristics and outcomes. These are mature people who can make balanced decisions about what they want while helping others do the same.

The next group of people are *control-oriented*, in the lingo of SDT. Instead of seeking out situations that will stimulate their intrinsic motivation, control-oriented people try to figure out the reward structure of situations, in order to conform to the rules of reinforcement they are playing by. When offered a new job, they ask, "Will I make more at this position?" They are more attuned to external factors, and less attuned to what they might actually want to do, putting aside such feelings for now. It is as if they are operating as agents without free choice, doing what they have to, given their belief that their outcomes are largely externally determined. Control orientation is correlated with some kinds of success, but it is also correlated with cheating and immorality. These are immature people who are able to get some of what they are supposed to want, but only by sacrificing their autonomy and by putting their integrity and their relationships with others at risk.

Finally, there are the *impersonally oriented* people, who feel helpless, as if they think they can't make much of anything happen. When offered a new job, they think, "What if I can't live up to the new responsibility?" They tend to be unmotivated and ineffective. It is as if they are operating without a sense of agency. Impersonal orientation is correlated with every kind of negative characteristic and outcome you can think of—depression, anxiety, poor physical health, and even psychosis. These are profoundly dispirited people who not only can't behave freely, but can't even be effective as pawns being controlled by something or someone else. They have largely given up.

These three causality orientations help illustrate the potential danger of accepting determinism as a guiding belief system or life philosophy (as described in Chapter 1). Those who reject determinism and embrace free choice (via an autonomy orientation) thrive. Those who somewhat accept determinism (via a control orientation), and try to work around the edges of it, do not fare nearly as well. And those who fully embrace determinism—via an impersonal orientation—feel helpless, as though they have no power or self-agency at all. For impersonally oriented people, the idea that their behavior is caused by forces they can't affect has become their (unfortunate) reality. Believing makes it so.

As we've seen, SDT has approached issues of psychological autonomy from many different angles and has provided a wealth of research support in favor of the claim that feeling autonomous and self-determined (rather than feeling determined by uncontrollable forces) is essential in human life, a genuine human need. However, SDT is not the only research tradition that emphasizes psychological autonomy as a critical factor in human flourishing. In fact, if we canvass classic and contemporary theories of positive personality development, looking across the areas of psychoanalytic, clinical, developmental, humanistic, and psychodynamic psychology, we find the same striking commonality across all of them.

Although many of Sigmund Freud's ideas have been discredited, he had many important insights. His most famous insight concerned the power of the unconscious mind. But Freud was also a pioneer of the idea that conscious processes play an important role in our minds by regulating emotions, controlling impulses, and dealing with the reality of the external world. Freud's word for this aspect of the mind was the *ego*, which mediated between primitive drives (the *id*) and the socially implanted (the *superego*, which SDT would say is the domain of introjected motivations). Freud viewed the ego as the decision-making component of the personality. It is connected to the sense of "I," which, ideally, is able to think rationally and in accordance with reality.

The main direction of personality development, according to Freud, is toward increasing power for the ego—hence his famous phrase "Where id was, ego shall be." The goal of psychoanalysis was to help people understand and resolve their nonconscious conflicts, thereby becoming the masters of their own lives. Though Freud did not use the term, it is clear that his conception of optimal ego functioning involved what SDT would call autonomy. As in SDT's conception of the self, Freud's ego regulates both down into the body, with its instincts and impulses, and out into the social world, with its norms and influences. Freud would have agreed that a better-functioning ego operates in a more autonomous way.

This idea was extended by the psychoanalytic theorists in the mid-twentieth century who developed *ego psychology*. Freud believed that humans were ultimately motivated by sexual and aggressive instincts. Heinz Hartmann, in the 1930s, thought there was room for more autonomy, in what he called the "conflict-free sphere of ego functions." Hartmann's version of the ego had the job not just of adapting to the environment, but also of shaping the environment as a free agent in its own right. Hartmann saw people's striving for greater ego autonomy not just as a helpful process, to be encouraged during therapy, but as the general cause of human development and social progress.

Other thinkers moved even further away from Freud while continuing to echo the same basic theme. Otto Rank had been a protégé of Freud's, but in the 1930s he created his own theories of personality development, creativity, and genius. He emphasized the will—"the integrated personality as an original creative force—that which acts, not merely reacts, upon the environment." According to Rank, great creators are able to disengage from the past, and even from their own prior beliefs, in order to achieve breakthroughs. He contrasted them with neurotic individuals, who are afraid to separate themselves from others or from their past, rejecting their responsibility to choose and create the world anew. For Rank, the self is a center of integrative activity, and ceding control to the world represents an abdication of our potential to change the world.

Erik Erikson, yet another Freudian offshoot, studied ego development across the life span. In the 1950s he created a very influential stage theory of personality development that considered autonomy a critical issue, especially in early childhood, as children learn to control themselves—using the toilet, clothing themselves, and quieting their temper. Each of Erikson's eight stages of personality development involves resolving a psychosocial crisis that characterizes that developmental stage. For toddlers, for example, the task is to embrace autonomy rather than falling into shame and doubt. This is Erikson's second stage (the first involves a baby learning to trust). Children who successfully resolve the second crisis have learned "I can control things," which sets the stage for the development of a solid sense of identity and purpose. Although autonomy is the primary focus for toddlers, it remains central to the remaining developmental stages as adults learn to do more and control more in their lives.

Building on Erikson's work, the psychologist James Marcia focused in the 1970s on the process by which people develop mature identities. He distinguished four identity statuses, ranging from a low level of development to higher levels. Movement through the stages requires self-directed exploration and reflection. In the ideal case, people are able to first move beyond a "foreclosed identity," that is, one which they have accepted without ever reflecting upon it ("I have to follow in my dad's footsteps"). Then they must move beyond a "diffused identity," where the identity is not yet firm (and some individuals have trouble committing to the self-directed exploration required to create one). Next is to move beyond "moratorium," in which the person is actively seeking a new basis for his or her own identity while experiencing doubt and anxiety. Finally people reach an "achieved identity," a solid sense of who they are and what is important to them, created by their own efforts. Marcia's theory says people find greater freedom of choice by developing hard-won knowledge of who they are, what they like, and who they want to become. The same basic theme can be seen in nearly all other theories of personality development, from Jane Loevinger's influential theory of ego development to Carl Rogers's theory of the fully functioning person to Abraham Maslow's theory of the self-actualizing personality.

When authorities try to control us, they often fail to achieve their ultimate goals. The parent who forces a child to practice the piano might ruin that child's musical motivation for life, or the boss who commands his employees might only breed resentment in them. But authorities often do succeed, at least in the short term. Even if our parents don't kindle an abiding love for music in us, they can at least make us sit on the piano bench for twenty minutes every day. We can even be controlling authorities to ourselves, as in the case of introjected motivations, in which we guilt ourselves into doing some task. Where is our "free choice" in such cases?

My position is that our ability to choose always remains, no matter what the situation, because ultimately, nobody decides our behavior but us. It is always our brains doing the computing and choosing, for our bodies, according to our priorities and values, as best as we can perceive these. Viktor Frankl, the Nazi prison camp survivor, claimed that no matter how terrible our circumstances, we have the capacity to choose our response to them, according to our heartfelt resolutions. This is the existential perspective boiled down to its essence.

Thus Tony could always choose to take the long shot—it was up to him, no matter what his coach was yelling from the sidelines. All in all, this is a good thing: it lets us think independently when we need to and keep sight of what we think is most important.

Of course, people may choose to give up in the face of onerous circumstances—to accept the belief that there is nothing they can do, thereby becoming fatalistic and resigned to their condition. And maybe such fatalism makes sense, especially when hostile people have the power of life or death over us—in such cases, going along with them may be better than suffering or dying. But Frankl's radical argument, which remains influential and inspirational today, was that we can even choose death rather than sacrificing our integrity and our values. Resistance is always a choice. Less dramatically, we can choose to speak out against the injustice we are seeing, to refuse to accept the way we're being treated by a coworker, or to radically alter our lifestyle based on new interests, intentions, or health goals. It just depends on what we care about, and whether we're willing to take the risks necessary to stand for what we think is right.

*   *   *

In this chapter, we've seen that free will is a *constant*—we always have it, even though exercising it may be very difficult at times. In contrast, psychological autonomy is a *variable*—it is how much we have learned to understand and accept our ability to choose. Some of us have faced and embraced this ability, whereas others may still be hiding or escaping from it. What we learn from SDT research is how important autonomy is for our well-being. As the late philosopher Lawrence Becker said, "Autonomous human lives have a dignity that is immeasurable, incommensurable, infinite, beyond price."[15] When we are aware of and embrace this truth, things go better for us. When we resign ourselves to being determined and controlled, we become just that.

CHAPTER 5

UNTANGLING THE MYSTERIES OF THE SYMBOLIC SELF

William James was one of the most important American thinkers of the nineteenth century. He contributed groundbreaking insights to both philosophy and psychology, including the question of whether free will exists. James's theory of the self is more than a hundred years old, but it continues to set the terms by which we define that essential yet slippery concept known as "the self."

James broke down the self into the "me" and the "I." The "me" is the self-concept, a relatively static belief system that we have about ourselves and the traits and characteristics that we possess. A particular person, for example, might believe that she is a go-getter, an extrovert, a conscientious person, a questioner of authority, and a person who is squeamish about bugs. When she fills out a personality questionnaire, she cues up this personal knowledge structure to answer the questions.

Notice that this "me"-based conception of the self lines up rather well with determinism because it doesn't presume that our self-concepts do anything. Maybe our "me's" are just a bunch of opinions, random nodes within our memory banks that don't control or even affect events. The "me" perspective also fits with the epiphenomenalist denial of free will, which says that self-experience is a mere side effect of the real action. Maybe, as the brain wetware does its thing, it naturally accumulates a misty cloud of beliefs about itself. But reductionists say that these beliefs are mere epiphenomenal effects of the brain processes that are really running things lower down in the hierarchy, rather than the causes or controllers of those processes.

James's "I," by contrast, is far from static. This aspect of the self feels conscious and active, feels itself to be operating the controls of its own mind. The "I" self has access to its beliefs about itself (its "me" features) and can draw these beliefs from its mind upon request (say, when filling out that personality questionnaire). But this self also has many other capabilities. It is the mental agent in charge of making choices and acting in the world. It executes the will—carrying out our wishes much like the executor of a will might, only doing so while we're alive to appreciate it!

Given its interest in understanding and supporting autonomous functioning, SDT's definition of the self is firmly in the "I" camp: it views the self as both a center of experience and the initiator and regulator of volitional behavior. In SDT the self is a process, not an entity, and can never itself be an object of perception (unlike the "me," which perceives itself as quiet, ambitious, creative, and so on). Within SDT, the self can only accomplish (or fail to accomplish) its functions of assimilation, integration, and choice.

While determinism focuses on the "me" side of the equation and SDT on the "I," both aspects of the self work in tandem in daily life. In an influential 1996 article, personality psychologist Dan McAdams coined a new verb—"selfing"—to describe this interaction: "what happens when 'I' encounters 'me.'"[1] Selfing, he wrote, is "the process by which people construct and animate a life-story, thereby giving themselves purpose, connection to others, and a basis for intelligent action." McAdams's definition reminds us that when we are trying to understand how a psychological process works, and why it works that way, we must consider its function. What problem does the feeling of being a psychological self help us solve, and what does it allow us to do?

In a paper published in 1997, and updated in 2017, personality psychologists Constantine Sedikides and John Skowronski attempted to answer these questions.[2] They summarized evidence for the idea that human beings have evolved a "symbolic self," which they defined as "the capacity of adult human beings to form a highly complex and abstract representation of their own personality and life-story, and to use this representation to help themselves in their own functioning." This capacity went beyond the capacities of prior hominids, and perhaps accounts for the eventual dominance of *Homo sapiens* over other *Homo* lineages. The symbolic-self capacity is built on language, and our desire to tell stories about ourselves and each other. It is also built on our desire to have a worthy, accurate, and defensible identity, and on our desire to be able to take charge and run things when necessary.

Sedikides and Skowronski viewed the symbolic self as a "third-order" form of awareness. It rests on the first-order ability to have subjective self-awareness, which is the simple capacity to distinguish between oneself and the world. Sedikides and Skowronski assumed that all vertebrates, and perhaps all living creatures, experience subjective self-awareness.[3]

Third-order awareness also rests on second-order awareness, often called objective self-awareness, which in turn is more complex than first-order awareness. Second-order awareness is the capacity to form a mental representation *about* the self, from outside of the self (as it were), which can be stored in memory. Objective self-awareness (that is, the ability to view oneself as an object) is generally demonstrated by the so-called mirror test. In this test, a mark is surreptitiously placed on a person's face before he or she is exposed to a mirror. Human children notice the mark around fifteen months of age—they've learned how they're supposed to look, and they know when that ain't it! Objective self-awareness is also involved in our ability to create a "generalized other" perspective in our minds, as when we think, "What if somebody else sees me picking my nose?!" This ability allows us to step outside our normal, more egocentric point of view and modify our behavior accordingly. Though seemingly simple, this second-order awareness capacity is something that we share with only a handful of species, including the great apes and likely a few other social animals with relatively large brains for their body weight, including elephants, dolphins, and crows.

The symbolic self takes this sort of self-recognition one step further, into third-order awareness, which involves the feeling of being me, living a story, playing my character in the world, deciding what to do next. The symbolic self is language based, multifaceted, and dynamic (that is, it changes over time). I and my colleagues described the symbolic self, in some 2012 research, as feeling like one is a character in a movie, making up the part as one goes along, guided by narrative structures both within the situation and within one's own evolving life-story.[4] Symbolic selves are suffused with a feeling of being "this particular person," and this feeling affects what we notice and respond to as well as what we choose to do.

Sedikides and Skowronski argued that one reason the symbolic self evolved in *Homo sapiens* is that it helped us interact effectively in complex human societies. The symbolic self is the face we present to the world, through which we try to get validation from others, as they try to get validation from us. In terms of the grand hierarchy, the symbolic self functions as the interface between our own body/mind system and other body/mind systems at the next level up; it presents our personalities to other personalities. We talking apes had to become very adept at presenting and projecting a persuasive yet agreeable "social character," moment to moment, within our ever-shifting soap operas. This ability allowed us to better negotiate alliances, attract and retain mates, resolve disputes, and much else.

A second important function of the symbolic self, according to Sedikides and Skowronski, is to defend itself against threats both internal and external. This is why we seek validation from others: we want to believe that the person that we think we are is legitimate and acceptable. Others always have the freedom to support, or perhaps thwart, this belief and desire, and when they do, we may get defensive—for good or for ill.

The third and perhaps most important function of the symbolic self, according to Sedikides and Skowronski, is to serve as an executive in the person's action system. The symbolic self "sets social or achievement goals…far into the future," "performs goal-guided behaviors," "evaluates the outcome of these behaviors," and then "links the outcomes to feelings regarding the symbolic self" (such as pride, self-esteem, or shame). In other words, these authors saw a role for the symbolic self in all parts of the TOTE process we discussed in Chapter 3 (test-operate-test-exit): that is, in setting goals (standard selection), evaluating discrepancies between current circumstances and standards (testing), and taking action to reduce discrepancies (operating). They also argued that outcomes of TOTE processes can feed back to affect the symbolic self, potentially altering its general feelings and beliefs about itself.

Suppose Tony took the difficult shot, but missed it. Bad move! After his coach makes him spend a couple of games on the bench, Tony may modify his sense of himself so that he doesn't always have to be the one who takes the important shot. Maybe he will even learn to strive for *assists*, in which he helps others to score. This might be better for both Tony and his team.

❧

Some readers may be wondering—what *is* this symbolic self exactly? What does it feel like? Can we catch ourselves being a symbolic self right now, in this moment? And why should we believe that this feeling, if we can find it, has any effect on our lives?

In some past writings, I have (somewhat contrarily) proposed that the momentary symbolic self is a "mental homunculus." In Latin, a homunculus is a "little man," and thus a mental homunculus is a little man (or person) that is somehow located inside a person's brain, perhaps running things behind the scenes. This was a tempting idea in ancient times. But within modern neuroscience and philosophy, the mental homunculus concept is usually thought of as a fallacy, a kind of logical error. The first problem with it is that there is no little man inside of people's brains, no tangible entity lurking behind the curtain; there are just complex waves of brain activity going on. Thus, using homunculus-type concepts to try to explain behavior is not often done.

Another problem with the concept of a mental homunculus, though, is that it seemingly tries to explain a phenomenon in terms of the very phenomenon it is supposed to explain—a kind of circular reasoning. Why did Johnny do X? Because Johnny's homunculus was trying to do X. How do we know Johnny's homunculus was trying to do X? Because Johnny was doing X. And a third problem with the homunculus concept is that it implies an "infinite regress," which is a logical problem in philosophy. If you say a little man in a person's head drives that person, then what drives that little man? It seems there must also be an even littler man inside the first little man's head, to drive the first little man. And then there must be a smaller man yet inside the second little man's head, and so on, ad infinitum. That takes you nowhere.

But no personality psychologist would claim that a mental homunculus is an actual second person that is somehow squatting inside of a person's head. Nor would one claim that there must be Russian-doll-type nested homunculi within our minds, going on forever. Instead they would say that there is merely a brain that tends to *think* of itself as a persistent psychological entity, and a tendency for that way of thinking to deliver better outcomes than not thinking that way.

At bottom, the homunculus may simply be a continually updated model of the person's underlying brain-state, which helps keep the brain abreast of its own current condition. In his brilliant 1999 book *The Feeling of What Happens*, Antonio Damasio explains this model in detail, saying that all organisms have the ability to create a representation of their own bodily condition (and in higher organisms, their mental condition).[5] This allows them to perceive that condition and take action to affect it (via TOTE loops). Damasio argued that human selves are uniquely complex because they are built upon autobiographical memory and upon verbal concepts and beliefs.

Still, verbal concepts and beliefs are only words, not realities. Thus, our self-models can sometimes be inaccurate, or even wholly false (as we'll see later). Maybe Tony isn't the next incarnation of LeBron James, as he likes to think! And this illustrates what I mean by the *fictional* homunculus—in that it can be made up of beliefs that aren't true. Still, when choice points come up, the current homunculus can have major influence. As the last to arrive on the scene, at the moment of choosing the way forward, it is the one who can say no (free won't) or yes (free will).

So again, what does it feel like to be a symbolic self? It's tricky, because it's like describing water to a fish—we can't see it because we're swimming in it. As the philosopher Thomas Metzinger says in his fascinating book *The Ego Tunnel*, we can't see the self because when we're looking for it, we're always immersed in it, inside a concentrated narrowing and focusing of thought that excludes much more than it includes.[6] We keep going into mental tunnels as we think our way through problems, and when we later emerge from them, we're oblivious to what we missed while we were gone.

The best way to realize what one's momentary mental homunculus is doing—to see things from outside the ego tunnel—is to lose that everyday feeling of "me being me." This can occur in dreams, when we suddenly turn into somebody else, or become something much larger. It can also occur under the influence of powerful psychedelics, such as LSD, psilocybin, or mescaline, or under the influence of prolonged sleep deprivation, or with intense meditation or spiritual practices. Such ego-transcendent explorations can be risky, but they can also provide very useful glimpses of the possibilities that lie beyond the ego tunnel. Only when our current self-beliefs dissolve might we see what is really there: boundless depths and infinite possibility. After such "peak" experiences, as described by Abraham Maslow, we may come back to a new and expanded everyday self.

My definition of the self as a shifting fictional homunculus shares some commonalities with the definition of the self in SDT, but they also diverge in important ways. The two perspectives are the same in viewing the self as the experienced center of activity and a means by which people control and regulate themselves. They are both "I"-type theories. The main difference is that in my version, "me's" are included, because the fictional homunculus thinks it is a thing. That is, it thinks it is a particular character in the world, which it is playing as in a movie. When we describe characters in movies, we describe their histories, their defining traits, their characteristics and propensities—we sum them up as people. And we do the same for ourselves.

The fictional homunculus then is a momentary "I" that thinks it is a longer-term "me." It is trying to better establish itself and its own story within its own mind. The homunculus is in one sense a mere hallucination created by our brains: there isn't really a "little man" in there, just extraordinarily complex brain processes. But the experience that we are a choosing self can have important consequences. This highest-level brain process, which tries to model and organize the whole show, can have top-down influences upon what's going on down in the machinery. After all, that's one of its main functions, in line with the ideas of Sedikides and Skowronski.

In all of this, storytelling plays a critical role. Symbolic selves are always embedded in narratives—in life-histories, in which there are befores and afters, and long-term themes and trends. What's more, these narratives are always changing with life's twists and turns. This means the self is always changing, too, at least in small or subtle ways. The self-version in charge at time t is not unconnected from past selves (except in extreme cases of dissociation or "multiple personality"); the different self-versions are all expressions of a common story that people tend to believe about themselves over time. Momentary symbolic selves are merely the latest incarnation of the person's attempts to organize and direct their own lives. These momentary selves remember their own histories and try to connect themselves to those histories, and they try to use this understanding in their decision-making. Like players in a giant video game, we continue to live our story, and to add to it, in the most satisfying ways we can.

To illustrate the critical importance of the self-narratives we live in, especially narratives expressing choice and free will, consider psychologist Jonathan Adler's remarkable 2011 study of how people achieve positive personality change during psychotherapy.[7] Study participants wrote personal narratives before beginning psychotherapy at a university clinic, describing who they thought they were and explaining why they were entering therapy. They also wrote twelve more narratives, one every month or so, about their changing sense of identity. In addition, their mental health was assessed at each of the twelve time points, via standard survey questionnaires.

After the study was over, Adler's research team content-coded more than three thousand participant-supplied narratives, focusing on two broad themes: agency (narratives that mentioned concepts like autonomy, choice, purpose, and mastery), and coherence (narratives that were logical, integrated, and detailed). The goal was to compare the two types of narratives in order to find out which type was more strongly associated with positive changes in the clients.

As an example of a high-agency narrative, one client wrote, near the end of therapy, "Being on my own is a scary place. At times, I feel like a little kid going somewhere for the first time—exciting, frustrating, wonderful, and scary all at once. There are a lot of changes in my life. I was feeling at their mercy, but now I see that I do have control. It's up to me to be able to stick with it and I will rise." This person had learned to take charge of their life, because nobody else would. As an example of a high-coherence narrative, another client wrote, "I am feeling like I was very lost for a very long time. Everything in my life revolved around everyone else and their needs rather than my own.... Therapy is giving me a chance to realize that I still have my self and it's helping me learn how to take care of myself first, even though it's really hard." This person had developed a new understanding of themselves, a new way of explaining their life to themselves.

Over the course of psychotherapy, the narrative agency scores increased for most of the participants. As a group, they came to feel more in charge in their lives—more like free agents, with the capacity to make choices and regulate their emotional and social lives. Yet the coherence of their narratives was unchanged; their stories didn't become more complex or more highly elaborated, as might have been expected. Yet they still experienced gains in mental health. Adler found that larger boosts in coded narrative agency over the course of the study were correlated with larger improvements in mental health as well as reductions in symptoms such as anxiety and depression. The more people learned to take charge of their narratives, compared to other study participants, the better they did. Greater elaboration in their narratives did not have the same effects. The point is to become the writer of one's story, not just to have a better story.

*   *   *

When we want to understand a psychological process, we often start by asking about its function. The symbolic self has many functions, from helping us communicate to helping us set goals or defend ourselves. But perhaps most consequential is its ability to grant us a sense of freedom and agency—the sense that we are "driving the car" of our lives. This sense of agency is critical to our well-being, as SDT research shows. But how do we know that our sense of being an agentic self is really real? How would we answer the determinist who claims that the mental homunculus is a delusion, that our feeling of making choices is all smoke and no fire? To answer these questions, we'll need to go a step lower in the grand hierarchy, to the functioning of the brain itself.

CHAPTER 6

FINDING THE SYMBOLIC SELF IN THE BRAIN

Researchers have been collecting data on brain activity for decades, starting with primitive electroencephalograms (EEGs). More recently, functional magnetic resonance imaging (fMRI) and positron emission tomography (PET) techniques have allowed them to chart and record broad patterns of neural activity sweeping across the various regions of the brain. These studies have made clear that the brain functions as a network, with complex patterns of connectivity occurring across and between different brain regions.

Researchers in cognitive neuroscience typically use such data to try to understand what brains are doing, especially when people engage in particular tasks—solving arithmetic problems, naming colors, or learning and recalling a name. Each of these tasks might produce a somewhat different pattern of activation, offering clues about how language works in the brain, or numerical problem-solving. But early researchers couldn't help noticing that people's brains remain continually active even when they aren't doing anything in particular. Even fierce concentration on some external task barely boosts our overall level of brain activity compared to our "resting" state. Either way, our brains keep using a large amount (about 20 percent) of our body's energy.

In the early 1990s, researchers gave this pattern of continuous brain activity a name: the default mode network, or DMN. The DMN is the baseline state to which our brains continually return.

DMN activity is marked by highly correlated activity across distinct brain regions, especially the medial temporal lobe, the medial prefrontal cortex, the posterior cingulate cortex, and parts of the parietal cortex. In DMN activity, these regions are sequentially activated and co-activated. Imagine a light show, like an aurora borealis, in which red flashes simultaneously in three areas of the sky, then green flashes in a different area, then blue in another area, then yellow in three other areas, and then red again in two of the same three areas—you get the idea. Sheets of activation are continuously sweeping across the brain like weather, but there is an organized pattern to them.[1]

When it was first discovered, DMN activity was thought to indicate that the mind is merely "wandering"—wasting time, not doing anything important, just daydreaming. Now, however, the DMN is thought to reflect very high-level control processes that involve many areas of the brain—a large-scale system in which the entire brain is being put to work via interacting networks of hubs and subsystems. In this view, the brain remains engaged in "internally generated thought" even when we aren't doing anything, and this self-generated thought can play an important role in our lives. DMN activity can include "mere daydreaming," in which we are idly musing with no purpose. But it also includes adaptive processes such as puzzling over the past, contemplating the future, and making plans in the present. Today, DMN is seen as a very healthy mode of brain functioning: it is far more than empty musing.

Although research on the DMN is a relatively new and rapidly developing field, one thing is becoming clear: that the DMN may actually provide the "neurological basis for the self," as brain researcher Jessica Andrews-Hanna put it.[2] In Andrews-Hanna's view, the DMN is the brain's feeling of being itself, its way of thinking through its situation and possible actions on a moment-to-moment basis.

Supporting the idea that it is involved in healthy functioning, the DMN becomes disrupted in many kinds of mental disorders. When people experience depression, psychosis, or post-traumatic stress disorder (among other pathologies), their brain's ability to host this high-level state of cross-correlated neural activity becomes impaired.[3] Important brain regions, such as the posterior cingulate and the hippocampus, start to "drop out" of the DMN conversation. They become less activated, or less connected to each other, than is typical in a healthy individual; the network breaks down. Impaired DMN activity is now viewed as an early marker for looming brain diseases such as Alzheimer's.[4]

To better connect the self and the DMN, let's return to Constantine Sedikides and John Skowronski's 1997 conception of the symbolic self from Chapter 5. These authors argued that the symbolic self is an adaptation that was so useful that it became part of every human's mental repertoire, and they ascribed three basic functions to the symbolic self: projecting a social face to interact with other selves in the social world; defending that face and trying to affirm its reality; and serving as an executive within a person's action system by selecting, monitoring, and adjusting goals and plans. Recall also that in a fourth function of the symbolic self, which those authors did not describe but I have noted, it attempts to represent both its own current state and its longer-term needs and potentials, within a person's consciousness of the present moment, as accurately as possible.

Might the DMN actually *be* the symbolic self? There's good evidence to suggest this could be the case. Imaging studies, for example, show that the DMN is especially active when people are asked to engage in "internally directed thought" or "internal mentation," such as remembering back to a particular time in their lives, considering how best to describe themselves, or reflecting about their own preferences. When we are thinking about ourselves, our DMN is operating. The DMN is also active when we locate ourselves in time—remembering back to the past, imagining the future, or thinking up stories that connect them.[5] Intriguingly, stories don't have to be our own in order to activate the DMN: when we watch a movie or read a novel, the same critical brain regions become more correlated in their activity, along with peripheral systems supporting the formation of complex new memories. It seems that the DMN is piecing together information across time to assemble narrative arcs that connect the past to the present, and the present to the future. And it isn't necessarily distinguishing between its own and others' stories.

If the symbolic self *is* the DMN, then, logically, we should find DMN activation when the symbolic self is performing its various functions. Let's consider the first of the three functions, according to Sedikides and Skowronski: that of interfacing with other selves. Is the DMN active when we're playing our parts within the social world? Apparently so. Research data show that the DMN is active not only when we are thinking about ourselves, but also when we are thinking about others, trying to perceive and understand them.[6] Specifically, the DMN is involved in our "theory of mind" computations, which give us insights into the mental states of other agents. It is also involved in our experiences of empathy, in which we put ourselves into the figurative shoes of others to feel (or try to feel) as they do. It is involved in our moral reasoning, too, and in our considerations of social categories, as we try to determine what is right and who is justified in situations of conflict. The list of social-cognitive functions that the DMN organizes goes on and on.[7]

The neuroscientists Istvan Molnar-Szakacs and Lucina Uddin proposed in 2013 that the DMN allows for "embodied simulation," which is a way of gaining insights into our own and other people's mental states. Their data suggested that we use our own reflected experiences to simulate the experiences of others. By asking ourselves, "What am I feeling right now?," we are more able to accurately assess what others might be experiencing. But it cuts both ways: by observing how others seem to be feeling, we get new information about how we are feeling. Embodied simulation allows us to use "high-level conceptual information to make inferences about the mental states of self and others." And "these mechanisms," they said, "work together to provide a coherent representation of the self and by extension, of others."[8]

In their comprehensive review article, Molnar-Szakacs and Uddin also discussed mirror neurons, which are a special type of neuron discovered in the 1980s. Mirror neurons are activated both when we do a particular action and when we watch others do that action. They respond to activity by any human agent, whether it is the self or someone else. Such neurons are assumed to provide a major basis for empathy, imitation, and social coordination. In Molnar-Szakacs and Uddin's view, mirror neurons are being put to work, by the embodied simulation process, to continually update complex models of both ourselves and others.

These and related findings suggest that our ability to construct and understand our *own* point of view might ultimately be based on our ability to model *others'* points of view. In order to present ourselves effectively to others, we had to learn to guess what *they* might be thinking. This capacity, once developed, could then be turned back onto the self, allowing us to better realize what *we* are thinking.

This is an intriguing idea with a very long history. It goes back to the American social psychologist George Herbert Mead, who proposed the idea of the "generalized other" in the 1930s. The generalized other is the external perspective that we learn to create in our own minds as children.[9] This external perspective can represent a particular individual's perspective that the person imagines within a particular situation ("what my mom would say"), or it could be more generalized ("what most others would say"). The point is that being able to construct self-alien perspectives, as needed, is critical for our cognitive functioning. In the early twentieth century, a Russian psychologist, Lev Vygotsky, argued that the human mind is built upon this ability to take the mental perspective of others.[10] The generalized other lets us escape our own ruts to make leaps forward. It provides a reality check, helping to keep our ideas consistent with what most others believe.

The DMN also appears to have an important role in Sedikides and Skowronski's critical third function of the symbolic self: that of running and regulating our action systems, and thus helping us set goals and monitor our behavior.[11] When participants are left to think alone in an fMRI machine, they enter a DMN state. When they are interrupted and asked what they were thinking about or imagining, they often report thinking about that day's goals and activities, or their plans for the future, or the possible outcomes of various actions they might take. Actually, the notion that people are intrinsically caught up in action-planning even when they aren't doing anything is an old idea in motivational psychology. It goes back at least to psychologist Eric Klinger's 1971 concept of "current concerns," the issues and wants that a person is currently thinking about, which occupy their minds and shape their perceptions of the world.[12] Klinger showed that current concerns are more than mere daydreaming; they are how we think about what to do next, and they are important.

Andrews-Hanna noted what she called an "intriguing possibility" in 2012: "that engaging in spontaneous DMN thought may allow individuals to construct and simulate alternative scenarios, mentally organize their plans, and prepare for what may lie ahead."[13] Here, readers should recognize echoes of philosopher Christian List's three capacities that are necessary for free will. An intelligent control system considers alternatives, selects a particular alternative, and organizes subsequent action. Maybe the DMN is the physical manifestation of the free-will capacity that List was discussing.

But if the DMN is most active when we are doing nothing, then how is it supposed to be integrally involved in our free behavior? This is an important question, because early theories of the DMN focused on it as a baseline, to which we continuously return—hence the word "default" in the name. The main reason for this label was that the DMN is typically (but not always) inhibited when people are doing an experimental task. If the DMN is inhibited when people are behaving, how can it represent the operation of their free will?

It is true that DMN activity is susceptible to "task-induced deactivation"—that is, it is reduced when we're doing something specific. For example, when someone being imaged by fMRI is asked to thread a needle, the person's high-level DMN becomes less active even as the visual and motor cortices light up.[14] This is because the person is concentrating on a very narrow piece of the external world. Most of the kinds of laboratory tasks that are used in conjunction with brain-scanning experiments are of this variety. They are relatively simple and involve externally focused tasks (such as categorizing stimuli according to their color, or counting backward from 100 by 7s). When the participants are asked to complete tasks such as personality questionnaires, however—which require them to pull up information about themselves, or to consult their own emotions or preferences—then the DMN activity remains strong or resurfaces during moments of internal consultation.

One way to think about how the DMN is involved in executive functioning is to revisit the concept of a mental TOTE process. Again, this process first involves selecting goals or standards to use for self-regulation ("What do I want?"); then testing, to determine the nature of the discrepancy ("What is missing?"); operating, to reduce discrepancies between the present reality and the desired future goal state (taking action); testing again, to confirm that the discrepancy has been eliminated ("Am I there yet?"); and either operating again, if necessary, or exiting the TOTE loop.

This description seems to fit what we know about DMN activity. When people in the default mode are interrupted and asked what they were thinking about, they often report thinking about what they want. It seems reasonable that this kind of self-directed thought represents the brain's ongoing attempt to decide where to invest its body's energy, its attempt to set the next goals and standards for its action system to follow. In terms of Christian List's model of free will, it is the self-directed process of generating alternatives in order to choose between them.

Once an alternative is chosen, things change. Testing ("Am I there yet?") may or may not involve DMN activity, probably depending on the abstractness of the task. "Is the thread through the needle yet?" likely does not evoke the DMN, for example, but "Am I happy with my marriage yet?" likely does. When we are concentrating on a simple or low-level task like needle-threading, we go into autopilot in ways that do not require high-level monitoring. In this case, activation flows away from the monitoring system toward the lower-level behavioral systems that need bolstering. Some research shows that the more the DMN becomes deactivated during difficult (but still concrete) tasks, the more successful the person is in carrying out those tasks.[15]

When the task is completed, the final test occurs. We return to a broader perspective, asking, "Have I finished what I set out to do? How do I feel about what I have done? Can I now forget about the task, give up control, and let my mind roam freely once again?" Consistent with this depiction, research shows that the DMN becomes fully reactivated a fraction of a second after an experimental task is completed. We exit the tunnel and go back to our natural state of free-roaming mentation.

*   *   *

As we find out more about the highest levels of brain organization, we see that they are looking more and more like *us*, lurking behind the scenes. Perhaps the DMN and the symbolic self are the physical outside and the subjective inside of the same basic phenomenon. And, consistent with the notion of top-down causality, perhaps the symbolic self is the *controller* of the DMN. In 2008 Randy Buckner, Andrews-Hanna, and Daniel Schacter proposed an interesting "sentinel" hypothesis—that the DMN continually monitors the external environment, looking for significant unpredictable events.[16] It remains alert to what is happening around us in case we need to make sudden decisions or take action. In other words, the symbolic self is always watching and waiting in the wings. We are ready to step forward and assume control as necessary.

CHAPTER 7

THE PROBLEM OF TOO *MUCH* FREEDOM

We've seen that humans live inside of symbolic selves, which are tasked with making choices—they are the executives in our systems, free to do as they please within limits. But just because we're free doesn't mean we're smart! Part of freedom is the freedom to make mistakes. And mistakes are surely made—after all, the symbolic self exists in a world of ideas and narratives, of story lines and themes, of conflicts and confusions, that is layered on top of the neuronal world. Eminent philosopher Karl Popper and Nobel Prize–winning neuroscientist Sir John Eccles, in their influential book *The Self and Its Brain*, called this "World 2"—the world of psychological meaning that arises almost magically from "World 1," of physical wetware. The symbolic self uses mental processes (just as cells use chemistry, and brains use the body), but it is not just the predictable result of those factors: through its executive capacity, it influences what happens down in the machinery in the same way that a CEO's decisions influence what the workers do inside the corporation—even though the CEO doesn't know all of those workers personally.

The most curious thing is that to the extent that we are cut off from our physical machinery, like mental "ghosts," we are also somewhat cut *free* of that machinery. Our functional autonomy allows us to do almost any crazy thing that occurs to us in the moment, no matter how stupid or maladaptive it may be. We are even free to kill ourselves, the ultimate insult to our physical bodies.[1] As the organismically oriented psychiatrist Andras Angyal wrote in 1941, "The relative segregation of the symbolic self within the organism is perhaps the most vulnerable point of the human personality organization."[2] The problem, according to Angyal, is that we are easily fooled, confused, and deluded in our self-beliefs. We might think we're always moral or always kind, but our family might tell us otherwise. Or we might think going to medical school is a good idea, overlooking the fact that sick people make us uncomfortable. This is one of the existential dilemmas of radical free will: that our choices are always made with insufficient information about our actual nature and condition. No wonder we are sometimes afraid of our own freedom.

From this perspective, the trick for us, as symbolic selves, is to gain enough knowledge of our own underlying condition to make reasonably good choices for ourselves. Can the symbolic self adequately reflect its own totality? Can we "get back to the garden" (as in Joni Mitchell's "Woodstock") to regain contact with our own deeper natures?

Recall that the symbolic self has three basic functions, according to Constantine Sedikides and John Skowronski: to provide a social face that interfaces with others' faces in the social world; to defend that face against threats; and, perhaps most importantly, to operate and regulate the action system, selecting goals and standards for TOTE processes and monitoring their enactment. And a critical fourth function of the symbolic self, which is the focus of this chapter, is to accurately represent or model the deeper system from which it emerges. If the self is a model, it must be a model of something: as such, it could be an accurate and inclusive model, or it could be an inaccurate and even deluded model. After all, "the map is not the territory," in the famous words of the semantics theorist Alfred Korzybski. And if the map is too inaccurate, then a person may be unable to make wise choices for him- or herself. They are traveling with the wrong map.

Let's make the problem more concrete by going back to Tony. Let's again say that Tony is a "gunner," biased to shoot when he shouldn't—in part because he imagines himself as a future professional basketball player. That is his current theory of who he is and who he will become. But suppose Tony really doesn't have the athletic talent to make it that far; he is fooling himself. Further suppose that Tony's real talent lies elsewhere, in music. He half knows that he has musical talent, because singing has always come naturally to him, and his friends praise him when they hear him sing. But he has always assumed that music is a dead end. It won't bring him the money and fame he thinks he wants—only basketball can do that. Thus, Tony's musical talent languishes at present. He is not providing himself with the experiences he would need to develop that talent.

Tony's problem is that he has the functional autonomy to be ignorant of, and to ignore, his own deeper nature and potential. He is out of touch with himself, operating from a flawed self-theory and a value system favoring money and status. In his mind he is the next LeBron James. But this dubious narrative prevents him from developing a different narrative in which he could become a musician, affecting the lives of millions through the music he creates and performs. How are we to understand this disjunction between who Tony really is, underneath, and the symbolic self he merely thinks he is?

Perhaps the most profound development in research psychology over the past thirty years has been the now well-accepted distinction between "system 1" cognition and "system 2" cognition, fully described by Daniel Kahneman in his masterful 2011 book *Thinking, Fast and Slow*.[3]

The basic idea is that our brains have two minds. The first mind (system 1) evolved earlier and is found in all vertebrates. It is instinctive and emotional, the seat of our automatic reactions and associations. System 1 lets us do familiar tasks on autopilot (drive a car, zip our coat, brush our teeth) and gives us immediate impressions and impulses regarding the world. So system 1 is how we react before thinking. In some cases, it provides us with deep intuitions—but it can also reflect troubling prejudices and biases.

The second mind (system 2) evolved later and is found only in us humans, with our highly sophisticated cerebral cortexes, which are layered on top of the older brain systems. System 2 is deliberate and logical, the seat of reason. It is based on language and lets us do things like focus on particular stimuli we care about, solve multistep mathematical or logistical problems, or intentionally dig into our memories to recall a person's name. It also allows us to correct for our prejudices and biases, if and when we choose to do so.

The main difference between the two systems is that system 2 uses words and conscious thoughts to deliberately engage with problems, often in a series of rational steps. It is "slow." In contrast, system 1 is preverbal and "fast." It has to do with our automatic reactions, which tend to rule the day unless we overrule them—unless we use our "free won't," in Benjamin Libet's terms. And remember that higher-level processes in the grand hierarchy always operate more slowly than lower-level processes, and thus the symbolic self always arrives last on the scene. Further recall that the symbolic self is informed by its own life-story, by the cumulative history and type of person it feels itself to be. These facts suggest that symbolic selves live mostly in system 2: in the verbal world, the narrative world, the world of conscious intentions.

Kahneman tried to evoke the curious situation of the symbolic self, living up in system 2, by saying, "Ironically, I am my remembering self, and the self who does my living is like a stranger to me." This sentence profoundly describes the dilemma of being an entity that tries to solve problems in a sequential, language-based format—system 2—but also lives in a place deeper than that—system 1. In the very act of reflecting on itself, the remembering (symbolic) self cuts itself off from the preverbal (automatic) self, getting somewhat lost within a constricted "ego tunnel."

Of course, the system 2 self is at least influenced by system 1, because it continually finds itself with already-formed impressions and associations bubbling up from system 1. It doesn't create these, although often it had influence on them, via earlier choices (what we've called "self-conditioning"). Still, system 2 has the functional autonomy to overrule system 1, to overlook or ignore it. Tony currently lives in a symbolic self that affects the choices he makes ("I'm a future NBA star, so, nah, I won't take that music class—it might interfere with basketball"). This symbolic self prevents him from developing barely recognized talents within his personality, which include the talents languishing in system 1, such as his ear for music. In other words, his symbolic self is failing at its fourth function—that of accurately representing Tony's real values and potential so he can pursue appropriate goals.

For thirty years I've been studying the processes by which people set and pursue broad personal goals, as well as what happens after they achieve such goals. Unlike many psychological studies that focus participants narrowly on particular tasks, or ask them preset questions, my studies are often more open-ended, letting in more life, as it were. We start by asking participants to tell us what they're up to: what goals they're pursuing, or want to pursue, in the near future.[4] Despite their variety and subjectivity, we can still collect a great deal of quantitative data after participants select their goals, based on various ratings.

At the beginning of a period of time (often a college semester), in a typical study we might ask participants, "What goals will you be working on during this period of time?" After they list some goals, we ask them to commit to working on them and to do their best to complete them. They are almost always willing to try, because they like the idea of explicitly going after things they (think they) want. We then measure the internality of their motivation to pursue each goal (the same way I measured PCT through-hikers' intrinsic and identified motivations). As control variables, we also ask things such as how difficult the goals will be to achieve, how important they are, or what obstacles stand in the way. Very often, we also measure participants' current happiness level or sense of well-being at the beginning of the study—because we believe setting and working toward goals are an important means by which people pursue happiness.

Then we track participants' progress toward the goals over time. How much effort do they put in? How well do they do? What unexpected difficulties do they encounter? At the end of the study term, we measure whether they have actually achieved their goals, or, if not, how much progress they have made toward them. Did they get what they thought they wanted, when they listed their goals back in September or January? And how did that affect them psychologically—did achieving their goals make them healthier or happier than they were before, according to our measurements? Or, if they failed to achieve their goals, did this drag them down, leaving them worse off than when they started? Our aim in performing these studies isn't just to catalog the desires of undergraduates. It is to discover what kinds of goals actually work for boosting people's happiness levels—and for keeping them boosted— and to discover whether there are some kinds of goals people shouldn't bother setting and pursuing, because those goals are unlikely to affect their well-being in a positive way.

Notice that all three elements of Christian List's definition of free will are represented in our goal-study methodology. In deciding how to fill out the goal sheet, participants must first bring to mind and consider various alternatives. Then they write down some subset of those alternatives and form specific intentions about them. Finally, they have the capacity in the coming weeks to take action to approach the chosen alternatives (although they are not always successful in these actions). Personal goal studies, to which I have dedicated my research career, provide a perfect methodology for exploring free-will capacities.

But again, just because we always choose doesn't mean we always choose well. One of my earliest and most striking findings was that when people list goals to pursue, *they often write down goals they don't seem to want.* Their ratings of those goals indicate that they don't expect to enjoy pursuing them (intrinsic motivation), and don't really see value and meaning in them (identified motivation). It's as if they've selected the wrong goals.

This can easily happen, because in our personal goal studies we give participants almost no guidance on what to write down. They receive a blank sheet of paper that they have to fill in—not unlike life itself. Thus, their goal choices may be little more than guesses. And these guesses may be distorted by many different factors, including the (higher-level) social factors of what their friends and parents think is important, or what the culture tells them is important. Or they can be distorted by the inaccurate symbolic selves in which they are living—by their own self-delusions. Self-delusions reflect inaccurate theories we have about ourselves, that even our friends and family members could tell us are wrong. For example, Tony's best friend, Alain, may doubt Tony's NBA-star narrative and feel that Tony is making a mistake by devoting all his time and attention to basketball. But Alain may be reluctant to say anything—perhaps he's waiting for the right moment, or waiting for Tony to ask him what he thinks.

Setting goals is largely a system 2 process: people thinking deliberately about what they want, then committing those goals to words, perhaps on paper (or computer screen.) This verbal goal-setting process has considerable functional autonomy; it is not merely determined by lower-level processes, even including the person's own deeper preferences and desires, down in system 1. But this functional autonomy can make system 2 somewhat stupid. It is free to do what it doesn't want! In our research, we refer to goals that match and express a person's deeper or nonconscious interests, needs, and talents as "self-concordant."[5] Many of the goals that our research subjects set are "non-concordant"—they don't really fit the person who sets them, and thus aren't really wanted.

～つ

Here's another way to think about this problem. An important area of personality psychology investigates discrepancies between two kinds of motives: implicit and explicit.[6] Implicit motives affect what we automatically orient toward in life without even thinking about it. Maybe we gravitate toward situations where we can be high achievers, or where we can have close relationships with others, or maybe where we can have power over others. Implicit motives are derived from our past experiences and reinforcements, and probably also our genetics. We express our implicit motives automatically and nonconsciously, often without awareness.

Explicit motives are what we *say* we want—for example, in response to focused questions on a personality survey, or in a conversation with another person. It turns out that explicit motives can be heavily influenced by a desire to make a good impression on others (what we in psychology term *social desirability*). They can also be influenced by ignorance—the incorrect theories of ourselves that we have unwittingly accepted or failed to question. Because of these and other factors, what we *say* we want can be quite off base. Our explicit motives are free to be "out of touch" with our implicit motives.

To better understand the difference between these two types of motivation, it helps to think about how they are measured in a research study. Implicit motives are typically measured by asking people to write stories about ambiguous scenes. Later, the researchers carefully read and "content-code" the stories, looking for certain kinds of themes. In the process, each participant gets a score on each theme that is being coded.

Suppose a participant is shown a picture of two women in a scientific laboratory. This is one of the actual cards from the Picture Story Exercise (PSE), the modern version of the Thematic Apperception Test (TAT), which goes back to the 1940s.[7] When asked to speculate about what is happening in the scene, a person might "project" their implicit intimacy motivation into the story—saying that what the two women really want is to be close, but things keep getting in the way. This person would get a high score for an "implicit need for intimacy." Someone high in implicit achievement motivation might write the story differently, saying that the two women are competitors who are both applying for the same research grant—thus getting a higher score on "implicit need for achievement." What's important in these studies is that participants don't know what is being measured or how their stories will be coded and analyzed. They don't know that the stories they write are really about *them*, not about the people in the pictures. That's why the scoring can reveal nonconscious motivation.

Asking about explicit motivation is much simpler, of course: "Are you a person who cares a lot about achievement? About connecting with others? About having power over others?" In this case, participants can say whatever they want us (and probably themselves) to believe.

What we learn from such studies is that implicit and explicit motive measures are almost completely uncorrelated. They are nearly separate systems. It's as if people often think they want things, or at least say they want things, that they don't actually want. When it comes to knowing what we actually want and gravitate toward in the world, we can be quite clueless.

Today, it is generally understood that implicit motives are grounded in system 1 (our automatic and "fast" behavioral preferences), and explicit motives are grounded in system 2 (our considered and "slow" verbal preferences). Implicit motives are mostly nonconscious, because they are how we react before thinking. Explicit motives are mostly conscious, because they are how we react after thinking. Some degree of divergence between the two is typical—we can't be expected to know everything about ourselves. But implicit and explicit motives can also diverge to a very large extent. When this happens, it can be a sign that symbolic selves are deeply confused or deceived about who they really are and what they really want. In such a condition, it can be very hard to choose wisely. We are using the wrong map.

Researchers studying the relationships between implicit and explicit motivation generally compute a discrepancy score, defined as the difference between the implicit motive score and the explicit motive score. For example, suppose Tony doesn't really want to think of himself as interested in fame, power, and glory—he prefers to think of himself as a team player. In a self-report measure, his score on explicit need for power might be about average—right at the sample mean. He thinks he's about like everybody else. But suppose that when he writes stories in response to ambiguous pictures, a strong nonconscious interest in power is revealed ("One of the women is trying to think of ways to impress the other one and earn her loyalty"). On the implicit need for power, Tony's score might be a standard deviation above the sample mean. That deviation would represent the degree of discrepancy between his implicit and explicit power motives. It would also indicate the extent to which his functional autonomy, in system 2, has perhaps made him blind to his own automatic inclinations, down in system 1.

In my self-concordant goals research, however, we use a different and simpler measurement strategy. We ask participants, "Why are you pursuing each of the goals you have written down?" We assume that an important symptom of self-concordance—of a good match between nonconscious and conscious motives—is that well-matched goals are pursued for more internal or autonomous reasons, because the person really enjoys them (intrinsic motivation), and/or thinks they're so important that they don't always have to be enjoyable (identified motivation). Such goals "feel right," and are pursued with no felt resistance. In contrast, non-concordant goals are the ones that feel controlled—ones we undertake because our parents want us to (external motivation), or that we have to guilt ourselves into pursuing (introjected motivation). To be highly self-concordant in one's life-goals is to have lots of the first kind of motivation ("I want to"), and not much of the second kind of motivation ("I have to").

One of the most interesting things about this measure is that it involves the person's own reactions to the goal they have just written down. And even though people may not know directly what to want—how to fill in the blank page of life—they *can* know how they feel about what they *think* they want! System 1 supplies us with these emotional gut reactions, and participants can simply register them in their ratings.

Our assumption that people feel more internally motivated when pursuing goals that express their implicit or nonconscious motives has now been supported in many different experiments. In such studies, we randomly assign participants to write down just one type of goal (say, three goals focused on achievement, or three goals focused on intimacy). Such studies find that if the assigned goal-type *matches* participants' implicit motives, then they feel more self-concordant in pursuing that set of goals. If participants who are high in implicit achievement motivation happen to be assigned achievement goals, they will feel much better about those goals than about goals that do not match their implicit motivations—as if they can go after them with full assent and ownership. If they're assigned mismatched goals—such as intimacy goals—they will typically be less interested in them and feel less of a sense of identification with them.[8]

Does it matter whether our system 2 goals match our system 1 inclinations? Yes! The benefits of felt self-concordance are many. First, self-concordant strivers demonstrate sustained energy and persistence in pursuing their goals. They keep going despite setbacks, and they are more likely to achieve their goals in the long term. Their goals express their deepest, most enduring interests; their goals matter to them, and they keep mattering to them, and thus they do what it takes to reach them. Second, when they finally achieve their goals, happiness levels increase to a greater extent for such people, and that happiness boost is more likely to last than it would if the goals were mismatched.[9] The PCT through-hikers who developed stronger identified motivation during their hike were both more likely to complete the hike and more likely to derive joy from that achievement.

Selecting self-concordant goals may not always be as hard as I've depicted—many people *do* know, or learn over time, how to correctly intuit what they like and are good at. I am lucky to count myself within this camp (I think!). But a surprising number of people are in the opposite camp, living in empty delusions about what is important, and in mistaken theories about who they are. These mistaken narratives can limit their beliefs about what they can make of their lives and keep them in ignorance of what will bring them meaning and joy.

So how can we learn to choose more fulfilling goals, so that we don't waste decades doing things we don't really care about? And how can we lessen the gap between our implicit and explicit motivations—that is, between system 1 and system 2?

One well-established technique is to engage in mindfulness meditation, in which you try to pay attention to what is emerging from within your mind *before* interpreting that information. In cultivating mindfulness, system 2 says, in effect, "Let me really watch what is happening in system 1, and not just assume that I already know everything about myself." By practicing this kind of meditation, a person learns to notice very subtle signals of what is going on inside of them (fleeting thoughts, momentary emotional reactions, a quickening of the heartbeat), and can then take them into account when making choices. Practicing mindfulness meditation can help

the symbolic self become less cut off from its own deeper personality, enabling it to do a better job of representing that
personality. The ghost becomes a better mirror of its own
machine.

Another way to learn how to make better choices is to ask
other people, who know us well, what they think might be
good for us, an approach proposed by the psychologist Tim
Wilson in his excellent 2000 book *Strangers to Ourselves*.[10]
Close others, in many ways, know us better than we know
ourselves. They may be able to see aspects of us that we are
currently blind to, or that we have been giving insufficient
weight in our calculations.

Recall Alain, Tony's friend on the college basketball team,
who knows that Tony doesn't have NBA-level basketball talent. What if Tony were to ask Alain, in some spontaneous moment, what he thinks about Tony's professional chances? Tony
may not like the answer he gets, but hearing Alain's answer
("Dude, I don't think so") may help to jump-start a process
in which Tony begins to consider careers besides basketball.
Alain might even get Tony to start thinking about where
his musical talents might take him. Maybe, in the end, Tony
would decide to embrace music.

Another technique for learning what to want—which
goals to pursue—is to think about why we'd pursue the goal
before we commit to it, not afterward. One reason that we, like
Tony, sometimes hold on to discordant goals is that the fact of
having made a decision—any kind of decision—has powerful
psychological effects, making us feel as if we can't turn back.
In his model of action phases, psychologist Peter Gollwitzer

refers to this as a "Rubicon," after the river that Julius Caesar crossed, marking the moment at which the Roman Civil War could no longer be avoided.[11] Gollwitzer's Rubicon model summarizes his decades of research on the difference between how we think before we make a decision and how we think afterward.

The model says that before we make decisions, in the "choosing" phase, we are in a "deliberative" mindset. We think carefully about our possible choices, gather information, weigh pros and cons. We're not yet ready to commit, and we're trying to be sure we'll make the right decision.

But after we make the decision, "crossing the Rubicon," everything changes. Commitment in hand, we are now in the "implemental" mindset. We think about plans, considering specific ways to get what we want. We also defend our decisions, trying to persuade ourselves they were the right ones. We engage in "post-decisional dissonance reduction," trying to avoid the thought "What if I chose wrongly?" At this point we'd rather assume we've chosen rightly, and forge ahead.

In my self-concordance research, my colleagues and I typically ask people to first list a set of goals, and *then* rate why they are pursuing those goals. Their goal selections are a done deal by the point they rate their motivations—participants have already "crossed the Rubicon."

In a 2019 experiment, however, we flipped this script.[12] There were two conditions in the experiment. In the first condition, participants first picked three out of six "candidate" goals, which they committed to pursue over the course of the semester. The goals we offered to candidates had been carefully selected to be either "intrinsic" in content—concerned with growing, and with helping and connecting with others—or "extrinsic" in content, concerning money, status, and appearance. Past research shows that intrinsic goals promote happiness and well-being, while extrinsic goals are unrelated to, or even negatively related to, happiness and well-being (this is the basis of SDT's fourth mini-theory, *goal contents theory*). After picking three goals, participants rated why they would pursue them. This is the typical setup in self-concordance research.

In the second condition, we reversed the order of operations: participants first rated why they *might* pursue all six of the candidate goals, and *then* chose three to pursue for the rest of the semester. This gave the second group of participants a chance to think about the possibilities before they had crossed the Rubicon of decision. In rating the goals, they had to ask themselves, "Why *would* I pursue candidate goal X? Because it looks interesting or meaningful, or because I feel some kind of pressure to pursue X?"

Participants in both conditions ended up with three chosen goals, but those in the second condition had to do more work, rating six goals rather than three. Was the extra work worth it?

Yes! And this is how we knew: as we predicted, participants asked to think about why they would pursue the goals *before* making their selections picked a greater percentage of intrinsic goals in their final set. Participants who did not get this opportunity ended up picking more extrinsic goals. And this turned out to make a difference in their lives outside of the study room. Although participants in the two conditions started out equally happy at the beginning of the semester (as you'd expect, given that they were randomly assigned to their condition), the participants in the "rate before choosing" condition, who picked more intrinsic goals to pursue, were significantly happier at the end of the semester than those in the "choose then rate" condition.

This technique is surprisingly simple and rather obvious, in retrospect: think about your motivations for doing a particular behavior before deciding whether to actually do it. It dials up an emotional gut check from system 1, helping you to realize what is most likely to be meaningful and rewarding. The key is to deliberate before implementing.

*   *   *

Goal-setting is one of the most important tasks we do as selves, and our ability to do it successfully is critically dependent on our ability to make the two parts of the self—William James's "me" and "I," or Daniel Kahneman's "system 1" and "system 2"—work together. This work isn't easy—truly knowing ourselves can be one of the hardest things for us humans to do, as pointed out by Socrates ("Know thyself") and by Benjamin Franklin ("Knowing oneself is harder than steel and diamond"), for example. But the results are worth the struggle. When we are able to avoid caving in to external pressures (real or imagined), or settling for shallow enticements, and instead manage to express our most heartfelt desires in our goals, then we find a deeper form of happiness and self-fulfillment. This is the purpose of our free will, and the promise of it.

I've talked a lot about happiness so far, but I haven't defined it. What is happiness? And how can we achieve such an elusive condition? It's to these questions that we now turn.

CHAPTER 8

WHAT BRINGS HAPPINESS

In order to study happiness in a research setting, we must find a way to measure it. Many non-psychologists I talk to balk when hearing this: "How can you possibly measure happiness!!??" they ask. "It seems so complex!" Actually, it is very easy to measure happiness (certainly compared to many other things psychologists measure). Psychologist Ed Diener, who essentially invented happiness research in the 1980s, defined happiness as a combination of three factors: feeling many or strong positive moods and emotions in life (positive affect); feeling few or weak negative moods and emotions (negative affect); and adjudging oneself generally content with one's life (life satisfaction).[1] When psychologists measure positive affect, negative affect, and life satisfaction, they always find that these three aspects of happiness are very highly correlated with each other (for negative affect, the correlation is negative).

This isn't always the case. A woman who takes in her grandchild while her daughter is in jail might incur extra negative affect (she suddenly must deal with a stubborn young child and the emotional fallout of her daughter's incarceration), but at the same time, experience greater life satisfaction (she feels that she can help this child, which is what really matters). Here, negative affect and life satisfaction might become elevated simultaneously—that is, the changes might be positively correlated, rather than negatively correlated. But mostly, the three facets track together so closely that they can be combined into one comprehensive measure—subjective well-being (SWB), which we'll often call "happiness." And this principle can be captured in a single formula: Happiness (SWB) = positive affect + life satisfaction – negative affect. To have high SWB means to feel many or strong positive emotional states (joy, inspiration, determination), to feel few or weak negative emotional states (shame, fear, hostility), and to be generally satisfied with one's life ("If I could live my life over, I would change nothing").

SWB is a major predictor of just about every positive outcome in life that you can imagine.[2] Happier people are physically healthier, have better immune functioning, have longer-lasting marriages, have more friends, make more money, and even live longer than less happy people. The list goes on and on. One might object here: "Of course, it's easy to feel happy when you are healthy, financially secure, and socially active!" In other words, might happiness just be a *result* of the fact that things are going so well for a person, rather than a *cause* of that person doing well? The research says not. People who manage to become happier than they were before (which may involve finding a fulfilling new job, entering a loving new marriage, or even having a near-death experience) subsequently improve their functioning across many other dimensions. Positive emotions help us in many ways, lubricating the gears of social interactions and giving us the confidence to try for what we want. The benefits of happiness are very well proven by the standards of psychological science.

Unfortunately, we can't scan someone's brain to determine what emotions they are feeling, or how satisfied they are with their lives. Thus, researchers must rely on participant self-reports in making their measurements. And that leaves us open to the same kind of skepticism that determinists have about the idea of free will ("Just because you feel free doesn't mean you are free!"). For example, some of you might be thinking: "Wait—just because a person reports high SWB doesn't mean their life is actually good! What if they are just deluded, self-deceived, or even intentionally oblivious to all the miseries of the world? What if their happiness is a myth, just as free will may be a myth?"

I'll just say this: If happiness *is* a delusion, then it is a very powerful and important delusion—one that makes a real difference in the quality of our lives (just like free will). And although it is true that a person could lie on a happiness questionnaire, by pretending to feel better than they really do (or worse than they really do), this happens much more rarely, and to a lesser degree, than you might think. Although there is always some quantifiable degree of error in the measurement (as there is in any research study), there really is a "there" there when it comes to measuring happiness. This "thereness" is demonstrated by the fact that there is quite good agreement across judges about a particular person's happiness level. If

John thinks he is happy (or unhappy), then so do his friends, his coworkers, and his family.

Even so, a skeptic might say, "Maybe John is just successfully projecting a false front, fooling others as well as himself, despite the fact that deep inside, he is really miserable." Maybe—but this would be very hard to pull off. Authentic happiness shows on our faces, and fake happiness doesn't. Others can see a long way into us, and they can see whether we're happy or not.

In the late nineteenth century, the French physiologist Guillaume Duchenne identified a special type of smile that all humans display. Duchenne smiles (as they're now called) are smiles that light up people's faces—not only do the corners of their mouths turn up, but their eyes and cheeks crinkle. We all know a Duchenne smile when we see one. And we all know that they only occur on the faces of people who are actually feeling the positive emotions their faces are expressing. They seem to have an "inner glow." Much research shows that we automatically like Duchenne smilers, and that we immediately trust them.[3]

People do often try to pose smiles, whether it's to be polite or to give a strategic impression of agreement. These "social smiles" are important tools in our arsenal—we all smile pleasantly when necessary. But the face knows, and the face shows! Perceivers can easily tell the difference between polite social smiles and truly genuine smiles. In a recent theory article, we argued that the ability to see this difference was selected for in humans (that is, it evolved in us) because genuine smiles give us important information—they are "honest signals" of how others really feel.[4] In evolutionary theory, an honest signal is a characteristic that unambiguously advertises health and fitness.[5] For example, a male peacock's particularly resplendent tail signals a particularly impressive animal, and furthermore, it's a signal that can't be faked, because the peacock must actually *be* that healthy to produce that tail. In our review article, my colleagues and I proposed that for humans, Duchenne smiles are honest signals of "a thriving lifestyle," a lifestyle that is providing many enjoyable and satisfying experiences. Duchenne smiles are honest in part because they are very hard to fake—they are difficult to produce unless the smiler is feeling strong positive emotion.

A few years ago, I started wondering whether a strong Duchenne smile might also signal a person's moral character. This question occurred to me because you rarely see pictures of "evil" people (such as Hitler or Stalin) displaying broad, open smiles. It's as if, despite their power, they have gone down a life path that doesn't provide warm satisfactions. The smiles they do show seem more like grimaces, smirks, or scowls than genuine displays of good feeling.

Psychology is a science, and so I needed to find an impartial way to test this intriguing idea. Here's what we did: From a large public database of Catholic priests accused of sexual offenses, we pulled together good-quality photographs of thirty-two priests actually convicted of such offenses—photographs that had been taken for their churches much earlier in their careers (before their convictions, but presumably after they'd begun behaving badly). All thirty-two priests were in priestly garb, and most displayed some sort of smile (or pained grimace!). We matched these thirty-two photographs with photographs of the priests who later replaced the convicted priests at their own churches, making for sixty-four photographs in all (the matched pairs allowed us to control for which particular diocese a priest came from). All sixty-four of the pictures showed head and chest shots of middle-aged men dressed in robes, posing for an official church photo. Preliminary data showed that there was no difference in the perceived ages of the two groups, which reflected the fact that the convicted priest photos were usually taken long before those men were convicted.

For the main studies we presented this set of sixty-four images to multiple samples of people, asking our participants two questions. The first time through the set we asked, "How happy does this priest look?" Participants rated each priest, one at a time. The second time through the set (with the photos presented in a different order), we asked, "Knowing that about half of these priests were actually convicted of sex offenses, which ones do you think were convicted?" Participants also made these yes-or-no judgments one at a time.

Across sample after sample, participants could tell, at a much better than chance rate, which faces belonged to the later-to-be-convicted priests, versus the replacement priests.[6]

How could they tell? Because the convicted priests didn't look as happy as the unconvicted (and unsuspected) priests, and exhibited less Duchenne smiling. Their smiles looked more pained, or ambivalent, or downright creepy. The convicted priests' apparent unhappiness statistically explained how participants could pick them out. Even though all these men were the same age and at the same career stage when the photos were taken, and even though the photos of the convicted priests were all taken long before they were even accused, our participants could already see that the later-to-be-convicted priests looked unhappy—which they took as a cue for inferring that those priests might be vulnerable to behaving in a criminal way. And our "signal detection theory" analyses showed that they tended to be correct in these judgments.

In our 2019 article we also found the same pattern of effects in a different set of pictures, of people being arraigned for a variety of crimes compared to matched control pictures. This was a more conservative test, because some of the people being arraigned were likely innocent. Still, we found the same effect, proving that it wasn't unique to the priest data set. I would expect to find the same effect for bankers convicted of insider trading, or for lawyers who have been disbarred, or for athletes who have been caught cheating.

In short, our recent research suggests that "evil" (or at least an immoral lifestyle) shows in people's faces to a detectable extent. But, of course, these were very unusual samples of images. Can we predict the self-reported SWB of ordinary people just from their facial photographs? Yes! In one study we asked college participants to take "selfies" while taking a survey and to upload those selfies. We also asked them to rate their own current mood. Later we asked judges, blind to the participants' self-rated SWB, to rate the Duchenne smiling displayed in those selfies. And it turned out that the judges'

ratings of the Duchenne smiling displayed in participants' selfies positively correlated with participants' self-reported positive affect, and again, at far greater than chance levels. The
stronger their self-reported positive affect, the more genuine
the smile in the selfie—the more it glowed. Happiness is expressed in our bodies—and other people can see it.

So, if authentic happiness can't be faked, then how can we get
the real thing? What's the key?

The Catholic priest study, which shows that moral character is written on people's faces in the form of Duchenne smiles,
supplied an important hint. Maybe, to be happy, one must be
a good person—a person who pursues virtue, connection, and
contribution, who lives an ethical and honest life, and who
doesn't succumb to base pleasures.

This is actually a very old idea, going back to Aristotle, the
ancient Greek philosopher. In his famous *Nicomachean Ethics*,
Aristotle said we should pursue *eudaimonia*—and if we did,
then happiness and good feelings would follow.[7] He described
eudaimonia as "activity of the soul in accord with virtue."
Eudaimonia shares some things in common with happiness,
and it is sometimes translated in that way, but it has a strong
moral valence. As Aristotle put it, "The happy life is thought
to be one of excellence; now an excellent life requires exertion
and does not consist in amusement. If Eudaimonia, or happiness, is activity in accordance with excellence, it is reasonable that it should be in accordance with the best within us."
This excellence, he warned, is "not an act but a habit; the good

of man is a working of the soul in the way of excellence in a complete life." For Aristotle, eudaimonia was the highest human good—the only human good that was desirable for its own sake (as an end in itself) rather than for the sake of something else (as a means toward some other end). Aristotle also said that good feelings came as a natural result of pursuing the good. He believed that people were rewarded emotionally when they behaved virtuously.

Eudaimonia remained a philosophical concept for thousands of years. But starting about thirty years ago, psychologists began to use the term to address what seemed to be a blind spot in existing happiness research. As these psychologists pointed out, we don't tell our children to pursue positive emotions—we tell them to pursue excellence, perhaps assuming (like Aristotle) that positive feelings will follow. The point isn't to feel good, it's to do well! Aristotle's concept of eudaimonia tries to describe what excellent functioning really is. Perhaps, by bringing the concept of eudaimonia into psychology, these researchers thought, we could usefully broaden our idea of what true happiness means.

Unfortunately, in modern positive psychology research, the concept of eudaimonia has become *too* broad. It is now an umbrella term that can stand for almost any positive-sounding activity, value, trait, or practice that the researcher cares to name and study. Frank Martela and I reviewed this literature in 2019 and showed that the concepts of eudaimonia or eudaimonic well-being had already been measured in more than one hundred different ways, and the list keeps getting longer.[8] Eudaimonia has been measured as being mindful, as having emotional stability, as having a sense of coherence, as being a helper of strangers, as being interested in self-realization, as doing new things, as caring about learning, as being serene, as being resilient, and much else. Eudaimonia is now a very big basket, and it is growing bigger all the time—perhaps to the detriment of science.

Martela and I wanted to find a way to circumscribe the concept of eudaimonia—to identify its essence, and to eliminate activities and values that do not partake of that essence. Philosophers have long labored, and continue to labor, to identify the conceptual essence of eudaimonia, and they have come up with ever more sophisticated logical arguments for or against a particular definition.[9]

In our review article, Martela and I took a different route, proposing a *data*-based route to understanding the essence of eudaimonia. We argued that SWB should serve as the empirical criterion for establishing which behaviors are eudaimonic and which ones aren't. In accordance with Aristotle's idea that truly eudaimonic (or virtuous) behaviors bring good feelings as a kind of side effect, we proposed that if something makes people genuinely happy, it is probably a eudaimonic behavior. According to this perspective, our own deeper natures reward us with positive emotions when we manage to make eudaimonic choices, because our deepest natures tend to be biased toward growth, connection, and adaptation. As shown by psychologist Dacher Keltner in his book *Born to Be Good*, humans evolved to be cooperative, to laugh and love, and to make culture, art, and music (in supportive conditions).

When we express these potentials, we feel happiness.[10] When we fail to express them, we don't.

Armed with this idea, we considered the published data. We wanted to find data in which participants adopted some kind of new activity that boosted their SWB. We also sought evidence that their SWB then stayed boosted over time. Aristotle said that eudaimonia was like a habit of excellence, not just a momentary amusement. This means that if the activity only delivers a transient mood spike (like riding a roller coaster or having good sex), it shouldn't count. A truly eudaimonic activity will provide more lasting benefits.

The graph on the next page illustrates the pattern we were looking for. It shows a prototypical person who starts doing something new at a particular point in time, thereafter achieving (and maintaining) a new level of SWB. They still have moods (small transient changes in affect), but these now fluctuate around a higher baseline—they have "transcended their happiness set point" (or at least managed to get themselves into the top part of their "set range" of happiness). The mindfulness meditation they now do every day, their new attempts to be positive and compassionate with other people, the efforts they make to feel gratitude and express it to others—these activities provide novel satisfactions, causing them to be rewarded with new positive feelings and to keep doing those activities. A new "habit of excellence" has been acquired that is self-sustaining because it is reinforced by positive emotions. And, in principle, the new and higher SWB baseline should be maintainable as long as the satisfying new experiences keep coming in, and as long as the person doesn't start taking them for granted (this is called *hedonic adaptation*).

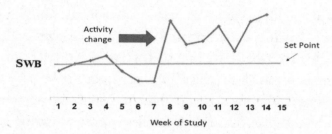

Happiness over fifteen weeks, courtesy of Kennon M. Sheldon

Martela and I also considered an additional question in our review article: What *explains* why a new activity causes new SWB? To address this question, we returned to SDT.

We've considered four mini-theories in SDT so far. But perhaps the most important mini-theory in the discipline, not yet covered, is *basic psychological needs theory* (BPN). This theory holds that human beings have evolved three basic psychological needs, defined as "kinds of experiences that all people need to have, in order to thrive and grow."[11] We've already talked about one of these needs, the need for autonomy: the need to feel that one chooses and causes one's own behavior, rather than feeling controlled by disagreeable internal or external forces. The need for autonomy is the "free-will instinct," and it prompts us to try to become more self-determining in our lives.

But SDT research also shows that we have at least two other basic needs beyond the need for autonomy: the need to feel that we are *competent* (that we can be effective, master new skills, and succeed at tasks), and the need to feel *related and connected* to important others (that we care about them, and they care about us). Sigmund Freud said that all humans need "love and work"—we need to have warm relationships and we need to be able to do well at tasks. SDT amends this by saying that the work should feel autonomous and self-chosen, not forced and compelled. An enslaved person may feel he is very good at what he does, but because the work is not an expression of his free choices, he will experience less satisfaction and a lower sense of subjective well-being than someone who feels both competent and autonomous. Indeed, a wealth of research demonstrates that the happiest people are those who feel competent *and* autonomous *and* connected to important others. All three needs must be met to arrive at peak SWB.[12]

Are there other psychological needs besides autonomy, competence, and relatedness? In a widely cited 2001 article we titled "What's Satisfying About Satisfying Events?," colleagues and I set out to answer this question.[13] We asked participants to identify "the most satisfying experience of their life," "of the past year," or "of the past week" (we ended up asking it all three ways). Once they had thought of such an experience, according to their own understanding and experience of the word "satisfying," we asked them to rate that experience according to a list of candidate psychological needs that we supplied them. We wanted to find out what participant-identified "most satisfying events" felt like, and whether those feelings fit SDT's claims about basic psychological human needs.

Our carefully considered list of ten candidate needs was taken from both classical and contemporary psychological need research and included SDT's autonomy, competence, and relatedness needs alongside other proposed needs in the psychological literature, namely, security, meaning, health, wealth, self-esteem, pleasure, and popularity or influence. After eliciting most satisfying events, we then measured how strongly each experience was felt during those events—Which candidate needs showed up the most? As a second test, we also measured how much SWB people felt during the events—which experiences predicted the highest SWB? What we found was that the same themes that were most present within satisfying experiences were also most predictive of the amount of SWB felt during those experiences.

Four types of satisfying experiences made the final list, including the three we'd expect from previous research in SDT: autonomy, competence, and relatedness. The fourth experience was self-esteem, thinking well of oneself as a person of worth. One study participant offered a typical example: "At my finishing college, I felt such pride that I had accomplished my goals, and I felt such loving support from my family." In this story, we see all three of the needs identified by SDT, as well as self-esteem—the person felt a sense of pride for having competently achieved autonomously set goals and enjoyed the camaraderie of family when celebrating that achievement.[14] Graduation, for this student, was clearly a eudaimonic activity centered on growth and connection.

To describe how eudaimonic activities lead to happiness and to include psychological needs in the picture, Martela and I proposed the Eudaimonic Activity Model (EAM) shown in the figure. The model makes a distinction between eudaimonic activity (doing well), on the one hand, and SWB (feeling well), on the other. This distinction causes endless contention within the well-being literature. Some researchers say that only eudaimonia is "real" happiness, given that it implicates virtue and that SWB seems shallower and more superficial than eudaimonia. Others say that only SWB is real happiness, because it is based on biologically rooted emotional responses that are hard to fake. Martela and I argued that doing well and feeling well are in fact both aspects of a more general concept: well-being (or "being well").

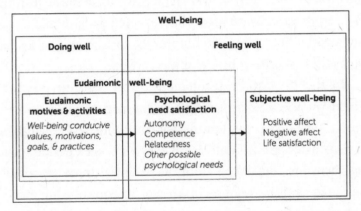

Eudaimonic Activity Model, courtesy of Martela and Sheldon 2019

The EAM also shows how eudaimonia and SWB causally relate to each other. Eudaimonic activities provide routes to happiness, just as Aristotle said. Specifically, eudaimonic pursuits bring happiness by satisfying basic psychological needs that are built into all human beings. As described in the model, new activities can lead to new satisfactions, which can then lead to new happiness. A leads to B leads to C.

This model is backed up by numerous studies. Chris Nie-miec, Rich Ryan, and Ed Deci examined predictors of in-creased SWB in the first year after students graduated.[15] How could these students get off on the best foot in their new lives? Students who rated either intrinsic aspirations (community, connection, growth) or extrinsic aspirations (appearance, money, status) as being important to them at the time of grad-uation tended to make those aspirations come true one year later. They moved toward what they said they wanted. But only students who pursued and achieved *intrinsic* aspirations had greater SWB at the end of the study than at the beginning. Making strides toward goals that reflected eudaimonic values had satisfied their needs for autonomy, competence, and relat-edness in that critical first year after college.

In the 1999 study I conducted with Andrew Elliot, in which we asked how picking self-concordant goals affected people over time, we found that attaining self-concordant goals boosted participants' SWB over a six-week period, mak-ing them happier. Why? Because attaining these personally treasured goals boosted their sense of autonomy, competence, and relatedness in their daily lives. Choosing goals that better represent one's deepest self helps to satisfy one's basic needs, which results in greater happiness.

In other research, my colleagues and I created a novel mea-sure of life-balance. "Life-balance," though much talked about within psychology, is often vaguely defined and measured. We introduced a measure based on how much the actual appor-tionment of time across different roles in people's lives matched their ideal apportionments.[16] According to this measure, to have a balanced life means doing many different things—working for pay, spending time with family or friends, pursuing hobbies and creative projects, participating in religious or spiritual activities—in the desired proportions. In our month-long study, participants who managed to create more balance in their lives reported increased SWB. This change could again be explained by the increased need-satisfaction in their lives.

In other research, we tested the effects of psychological authenticity upon need-satisfaction and measures of well-being.[17] To approach this question, we asked participants to rate their personality traits both "at a party" and "in an unguarded moment when you are with loved ones." We reasoned that the most authentic participants would be those who didn't differ very much in these two situations; in either case they wouldn't be playing a role, they would just be themselves. As expected, greater authenticity (lower discrepancy between the two situations) predicted higher SWB, which was again explained by higher levels of need-satisfaction.

In a way, the EAM provides a very simple prescription for happiness: try to spend your time doing things that bring you feelings of autonomy ("I really want to do this"), competence ("I'm doing it well and creatively"), and relatedness ("It's bringing me closer to others"). Spending your time this way will increase your SWB, which will then reinforce what you are doing, creating a virtuous cycle of positive change—even an "upward spiral," which is the holy grail, if there is one, in positive psychology research.[18]

So happiness is possible after all! But why, then, does the world seem so full of unhappy people? Why do we make so many poor choices, choices that lead us further from, rather than closer to, fulfillment? The answer we considered in the previous chapter was that as symbolic selves, who are making choices up in verbal system 2, we are to some extent free agents. We are partially cut off from the mental processes that support us down in system 1. Thus, we are free to choose poorly—and sometimes we do.

But a somewhat different answer, one not yet considered, is that we often have no idea how our choices will affect our emotional lives down the road. If we don't know how our choices will make us feel, how can we choose wisely?

This is one of the principal questions posed by what's known as *affective forecasting* research.[19] In such research, people are asked to predict how they will feel in the future after some event happens—including positive events, such as eating tasty food, receiving a monetary reward, getting a kiss from an admired person, or having one's preferred candidate win the election—and negative events, such as receiving bad news, experiencing a painful shock, or having one's candidate lose the election. Affective forecasting is like weather forecasting—we want our forecasts to be accurate so we can decide what to do. If we don't know what the weather will be, we can't plan the picnic, or the hike, with confidence. Affective forecasting is similar. If we don't know how we might feel after doing X, how can we be sure that choosing X is wise?

In a typical affective forecasting study, the researchers, after collecting the forecasts, make it so that the event actually happens. The participant really does find a five-dollar bill on the ground, or really does hear somebody make a sexist remark. Or the researchers tie the study to an actual upcoming event, such as an election. Then they measure study participants' emotional responses to that event after it has occurred. Affective forecasting errors are defined as the extent to which people "mispredict" the effects of the event on their emotions—such as how good or bad the event will make them feel, or how intense those feelings will be, or how long the feelings will last before fading away. In the previous chapter, we talked about discrepancies between implicit and explicit motives, and a moment ago, we talked about discrepancies between who we are in social settings versus intimate situations. Here, the discrepancies involve gaps between how we think we'll feel and how we really end up feeling after an event happens.

Affective forecasting research has shown that our ability to predict how we will feel in the future is surprisingly limited. We tend to overestimate how long good feelings will last (not as long as we think), and underestimate how quickly bad feelings will fade (faster than we think). Or we focus on the wrong things in making our predictions (such as how much the job pays instead of how much we will like doing it). Or maybe we focus on just one factor at the expense of other relevant factors. In comparing "living in the Midwest" to "living in California," for example, we might assume we'll be happier in California because we're only thinking about California's warm beaches. We can easily overlook the higher cost of living in California, or the increased danger of earthquakes or fires. Maybe places like Missouri aren't so bad after all.

Using the lens of affective forecasting research, we can again see that maybe our problem isn't that we aren't free—instead, it's that we don't know enough to use our freedom effectively.

In 2010, colleagues and I published a study exploring how affective forecasting errors affect the goals we choose to pursue.[20] We were trying to understand why people pursue extrinsic goals (such as becoming wealthy, famous, or beautiful), given that achieving these kinds of goals are known to be less satisfying than achieving intrinsic goals (growing as a person, having deep relationships, and serving one's community). In terms of the EAM, intrinsic goals are eudaimonic, exemplifying forward-looking attempts to connect and grow, and satisfying our deepest needs and making us happy as a result. Extrinsic goals are non-eudaimonic: they don't satisfy those deep needs, and in some cases can even interfere with a quest for fulfillment. Why do some people strongly endorse extrinsic goals if they aren't need-satisfying? What keeps them going back to a dry well?

In our study we found, as always, that people who favor extrinsic over intrinsic goals are less happy. But our main finding was that those same people *believed* (forecasted) that achieving extrinsic goals would bring them more happiness. Given the actual data, this was likely a delusion (a mistaken forecast).

In a second 2010 study, we randomly assigned participants to pursue goals of either an extrinsic type or an intrinsic type for a monthlong period (and yes, undergraduates are willing to try this!). At the end of the month, those who had achieved intrinsic goals were happier than they had been when they started. Those who achieved extrinsic goals got no happiness benefit at all. Even participants who at first strongly endorsed extrinsic values, when randomly assigned to the extrinsic-goals condition (the types of goals they said they wanted), didn't benefit from attaining such goals. It seems that extrinsic goals simply don't satisfy psychological needs, no matter what we might believe about them. Instead, in our study, even participants who strongly endorsed extrinsic values at the outset gained a greater sense of well-being when they achieved intrinsic goals assigned to them—something they did not predict or expect. And the sense of well-being they gained was just as great as it was for other participants in the intrinsic-goals condition.

The upshot is that people who orient toward money, status, and image overestimate the positive happiness effects of attaining these extrinsic goals and underestimate the positive effects of attaining intrinsic goals. This is because they are living with distorted beliefs about themselves and about the world: beliefs that do not encourage eudaimonic virtue, but instead encourage dominance and display. They are chasing delusions, seemingly unable to understand why they keep "doing the same thing, expecting different results" (the definition of insanity, a quote sometimes attributed to Albert Einstein).

But here's another possible reason for suboptimal choices: maybe people *do* know that intrinsic goals are more fulfilling, but they also think that such goals must be put off until a later time in their lives. In a 2018 study colleagues and I compared the goals and happiness levels of two types of people:

businesspeople (or business students) and artists (or art students).[21] Our reasoning was that by trying to maximize profit in an entrepreneurial endeavor, businesspeople, by definition, are focusing on extrinsic goals. Artists focus instead on intrinsic goals, by trying to maximize their creativity in a self-expressive endeavor. Of course, businesspeople may also find creative self-expression in the business world, and artists may also desire wealth or fame, so the distinction is not black-and-white. Still, in general, at their core the two vocations have very different focuses.

In a first study we confirmed (as expected) that the business students were more concerned with extrinsic (money-based) career goals and had more external (monetary-reward-based) reasons for pursuing those goals. Meanwhile, art students had fewer extrinsic goals and less external career motivation; they weren't thinking about money and rewards, they were thinking about making art. Yet when we asked both groups about their long-term goals, the answers looked very similar: both groups eventually wanted opportunities to grow as people, connect with others, and contribute to society. A second study replicated this pattern and revealed that business and art students also hoped to have similar levels of intrinsic motivation in their jobs in the future. Ultimately, both groups wanted careers that they were internally motivated to pursue.

These results suggested that at least some of those who are driven by external factors aren't deluded about what they want, but are making a calculated decision to put their intrinsic goals and motivations off until the long-term future. They want to amass their stash first, and then do what they really want. But is it a good bargain to put off fulfillment for years or decades? What if one never gets back around to one's true interests, or never feels that now is the right time to seek meaning? It's hard to say. But surely, some such people die unfulfilled—and they surely don't take their money with them.

Yet there's also room for hope in these findings. Maybe all humans know, in some deep way, what's really important, even if we aren't yet living those values. Maybe we all have a kind of "internal compass" that can point us toward the decisions that will be most satisfying and fulfilling.

The idea of an internal compass has a long history within psychology. The humanistic psychologist Carl Rogers referred to it as the organismic valuing process (OVP), which he defined as "the ability to judge experiences in terms of their value for promoting or hindering our actualization and growth."[22] According to Rogers, many people come to therapy because they live in a state of confusion: they have lost touch with their OVP, and as a result they do not know who they are or what they want. Often, they are caught up in beliefs about themselves that are inaccurate or overly limiting, based on the "conditions of worth" that were imposed on them as children ("You are only lovable if you are this kind of person") or are imposed on them to this day ("You are only lovable as my romantic partner if you are this kind of person"). The symbolic self they live in is out of touch with its underlying organism (perhaps like Tony).

Client-centered therapy, invented by Rogers in the 1950s, was designed to solve this problem. This humanistic type of therapy tries to provide clients with a safe environment in which to explore their problems, so they can become more "congruent." The therapist serves as both a mirror (reflecting back to clients what they are thinking, so they can learn to recognize and claim their own thoughts) and as a model (of how to live an authentic and open life). A successful course of therapy reconnects clients to their deeper feelings and creative potentials, helping them to overcome their stuck condition to resume growing and developing.

This is a comforting idea: that we are always capable of discovering (or rediscovering) what we really think and feel, and with the right kind of effort or reflection, we can gain access to that knowledge. Rogers's optimism was based on his assumption that people are naturally growth focused. Self-determination theory shares this optimism in holding that people are naturally oriented toward finding and developing intrinsic motivations. Both views illustrate the basic tenets of the organismic perspective, which views people as living systems that automatically seek and pursue increasing complexity and creativity.

Rogers also agreed with SDT that these self-organizational capacities can be fragile. Many people become stuck, or even regress, in their lives. Still, although people may lose access to their growth capacities, or fail to develop that access in the first place, the capacities always remain. As Abraham Maslow, one of the founders of humanistic psychology, put it in 1968, "The inner voice is not strong.... [I]t is weak and delicate and subtle and easily overcome by habit, cultural pressure, and wrong attitudes towards it. Even though weak, it rarely disappears."

Is it possible to scientifically test such an optimistic but nebulous idea as "the organismic valuing process"? In a 2003 article my colleagues and I tried to do just that by asking people to repeatedly rate the importance of both intrinsic and extrinsic values.[23] We took advantage of the fact that people don't just give the same answer every time they are asked the same question. They tend to move up or down a little in their ratings. Normally such variation is thought to be random, like noise or static, without any meaningful pattern. But we wondered whether, when people shifted, they shifted in a particular way—toward the goals shown by research to be healthier or to bring greater happiness. Such "biased shifts" wouldn't be just random; they would have direction—toward growth and health. Specifically, we tested the idea that when people modify or misremember their goals, they will have a nonconscious tendency to shift in the intrinsic direction.

We tested this idea in two ways: both by asking people to rate value statements repeatedly ("What do you think now, thirty minutes later?"), and by asking them to remember what they had said previously, in an earlier questionnaire ("How did you answer these questions before?"). Of course, most participants couldn't really remember what they said the first time through, so there was plenty of room for them to change, or to misremember, the ratings they had given the first time.

The first time through, participants endorsed intrinsic goals to a greater extent than they endorsed extrinsic goals. Again, this is a well-known finding—that, in general, people say they value community, growth, and service more than image, status, and money.

But we were more interested in what they would say the *second* time through. And, as predicted, there was a "biased shift." Whether our participants were merely remembering, or actually rethinking, their earlier responses, they tended to give even higher ratings to the intrinsic goals the second time around. It was as if their OVPs became activated by the chance to reconsider an earlier suboptimal judgment, which then helped them to improve those earlier judgments.

Most psychological research on cognitive biases finds that our biases are somewhat negative and unflattering—we exaggerate our own positive qualities (self-serving bias), we think more people agree with us than really do (false consensus bias), or we are prone to blame people for their misfortunes rather than considering their unfortunate situations (the fundamental attribution error). But in this study, we found evidence for a positive bias—one that could help explain why many people do manage to find happiness eventually (you may be surprised to learn that worldwide, the average SWB score is 7 on a scale of 1 to 10). The bias suggests that we know, nonconsciously, what will bring satisfaction, and that we can automatically move in that direction even if our symbolic selves aren't yet onboard. The organism can know, even if the self doesn't.

*   *   *

The task of changing one's life to become more virtuous and ethical, to live out one's most ideal values, may seem daunting. But our research shows that people have an innate propensity to orient toward such values, and to seek growth when their life-conditions support it (and sometimes even when they don't—the ability to do this is called *resilience*, and it's one of the key correlates of psychological health). The main thing we need to do is simply try! Just announcing our new intentions to others can make them seem more real to us—and when we begin to pursue intrinsic goals, we can start a virtuous cycle, where small changes lead to bigger changes, leading to even bigger changes—and leading, ultimately, to real happiness and fulfillment.

CHAPTER 9

THE DIGITAL SELF

Throughout this book, I have advocated for a particular idea: that human beings have free will in part because they live inside of symbolic selves. The symbolic self emerges from and is built upon brain processes but is not strictly determined by them. The self's job, as the spearhead of the organizational impulse within the mind, is to "take the reins of the brain"—to decide who the person is, what the person wants, and how to go after it. There could be no self without a brain, but once there is a self, it can have top-down effects on the operation of the brain—causing the activity of neurons at least as much as the neurons cause the activity of the self, in the same way the corporate CEO causes the activity of the workers as much as the workers cause the activity of the CEO.

I've also described the symbolic self as in part a simulation of the brain's underlying condition—a model that the brain is running of itself that has some capacity to take control of behavior. That model is informed by the objective conditions down in the body (Is the body hungry, tired, or agitated?), but it is also informed by the high-level self's current beliefs about itself and its current goals. A marathon runner nearing the finish line may feel desperately tired, and that person's body may badly want to stop running. But it is the self that is making the decisions, not the body, and thus inner reserves may yet be found in the body—reserves that can help the runner to make a final sprint and win the race. The body doesn't care, it only wants to rest—but the self does care, and it can make wonderful, magical things happen.

Now I want to push these ideas a bit further. If the symbolic self is in some ways a mental model, then could that model be further modeled by a computer program? In such a case, would the computer program actually feel like the self it is simulating—could it be conscious, could it care about things? And could the computer simulation of a person's self-process continue to run even after the person's death, supplying the world with the continued thoughts and judgments of that person? Even more intriguingly, *could a computer program develop its own symbolic self*? My tentative answer to all these questions is yes, eventually. But artificial personality is a brand-new field, and there is a long way to go.

Artificial intelligence (AI) itself is a relatively old field, dating to the 1950s, but until recently it had made only slow progress in demonstrating human-level intelligence. There are two main reasons for this: limitations on computing power, and the fact that earlier AI models took a logical and deductive approach. They were based on researchers' conceptual models of the human thought process, which the researchers tried to implement as rules programmed into software. In the past ten years or so, both limitations have been largely transcended.

Regarding the first limitation, Moore's law (which isn't actually a physical law, just a noticeable trend) states that every two years, advancing technology roughly doubles the amount of computing power available. This pattern has held consistent ever since Gordon Moore first pointed it out in 1965, although some think the process is slowing down because of quantum-scale limitations. In any case, we have much more computing power today than we had even ten years ago (specifically, 2^5 more, or 32 times more). These advances have contributed to large breakthroughs in AI.

Regarding the second limitation, recent AI research has largely given up on trying to understand human thought processes conceptually and instead embraced a brute-force "machine-learning" technique. The computer is unsupervised: it is turned loose to process huge amounts of data looking for deeply embedded patterns. It finds this knowledge through *induction*, by discovering patterns present in the data, rather than by *deduction*, using logic and theory to determine the patterns it should look for. Discovery of the deep patterns in the data allows the computer to find algorithms for predicting further outcomes and events, techniques it can apply to any new cases or situations presented to it. If "extremely complex result Y" almost always follows "extremely complex situation X," then when X is observed, that means Y is probably coming.

In an important sense, machine learning works just like a human brain. Human brains, too, are capable of assimilating large amounts of data and detecting subtle patterns in that data through induction and intuition (via system 1). The difference is that computers can handle vastly larger quantities of information than a human brain can, and thus such techniques have the potential to detect far more complex and subtler patterns than a human brain can detect. For example, AI systems have been used to crunch giant reams of medical data to arrive at the correct diagnosis of a patient's illness; to forecast future market trends based on analysis of past trends; to recognize particular faces within huge crowds; and to play complex games, such as chess and go, at levels of sophistication unreachable by human grandmasters.

Machine learning is also used every day by corporations and advertisers to predict what will make us buy, make us click, persuade us. Your Facebook feed, if you haven't noticed, is exquisitely tailored to your interests and beliefs—all with the goal of keeping you active on Facebook and buying the products that pop up onscreen.[1]

It is beyond the scope of this book to provide a thorough overview of AI technology, machine learning, neural networks, and the many ways that such networks can be trained. But I do want to speculate just a bit about whether, or how, an AI could simulate a self—or could even have a self itself. Christian List, the philosopher who analyzed free will in terms of three mental capacities (to consider alternatives, form intentions, and enact behavior), argued that intelligent control systems of any type (human or artificial) could have free will. Okay—so what would an artificial control system need to look like in order to perhaps have human-level sentience, and even free will?

There are several ways to think about the relationship of AI to personality and human behavior. One way is to use AI to create personality profiles of individual people. For example, the company Crystal has been using machine-learning techniques since 2015 to provide users with profiles of targeted people based on their LinkedIn pages and other publicly available data.[2] Users of Crystal's services theoretically gain a head start on knowing what a person is like and how to deal with that person. In another example, a 2020 Russian study showed that a machine-learning program, given data about the personality traits of a set of individuals as well as photographs of those same people, could learn to predict the trait profiles of new people just from their appearance, and it proved to be able to do so considerably better than human observers could. There were very subtle correspondences between appearance and traits, and the computer could learn them.[3]

This discussion might remind you of what we found in our Catholic priest pedophile study—that human observers could tell, at a better than chance rate, which priests would later be convicted of sex crimes, just based on their church website photos. People's personalities are written on their faces, and thus we can tell something about what people are like just by looking at pictures of them. The AI in the Russian study did something similar: it picked up on subtle kinds of information to develop a prediction algorithm (formula) that let it make very good guesses about new people it was shown. This algorithm could be fed a single random picture of you and then spit out a rather large amount of nearly correct guesses about who you are and what you are like.

One implication of such findings is that AIs could learn to identify actual criminals at a much better than chance rate simply based on the criminals' appearances. This implication is both scary and exhilarating at the same time. Should such information be allowed to dictate the amount of surveillance a person is under? Should it determine whether someone is prosecuted for a crime, or the length of a prison sentence? Should information derived from such AIs be admissible in court, to help convict or acquit people? These are difficult questions, but they illustrate just a few of the many ethical dilemmas posed by the rise of intelligent software. And they are not just fodder for dystopian novels: philosophers and legal scholars are beginning to think about them as well.[4]

AI can also go beyond just making inferences *about* a personality to actually acting *like* a personality. Apple's Siri, Amazon's Alexa, and Microsoft's Cortana are all attempts to give a veneer of personality to computer software—to make us feel like we are interacting with a person when we are interacting with computer code. These agent-based computer programs can extract semantic meaning from natural language (already a huge accomplishment) and are then able to riff off of this meaning in sophisticated ways to interact with human users. No matter what we say, they can say something back. They seem to be having a real conversation with us.

The point of such artificial personalities is to make us feel engaged with our computers. We can start to feel like they are more than mere machines—that they are, in some sense, people like us. Programmers try to give computed personalities appealing traits, such as being humble, helpful, playful, and even sassy. If we ask Siri a strange question and she makes a surprising joke, we like her. We relate to her. Then, perhaps, we are more likely to believe, trust, and share what she tells us.

But computer agents like Siri and Alexa are a long way from having sentient personalities. Most of us know that Siri is just a program, a set of techniques for generating responses that sound humanlike. Most of us aren't fooled—we know that Siri isn't real. Why? Because we can tell there is no inside there, no "feeling of being Siri" that we could come to know and appreciate, such that we might want to become friends with Siri as a fellow conscious entity in the universe.

In other words, Siri can't yet pass the *Turing test*. This test, first proposed by Alan Turing in 1950, says that if you can have an extended conversation with a computer program in which it convinces you it is a person (rather than a program), then the program has reached true human-level sentience.[5] More technically, the standard criterion (within Turing test competitions) is that if the computer can convince more than 30 percent of knowledgeable human judges that it is real, after a series of five-minute keyboard conversations, then it has passed the test.

This seems like a rather low bar, if you think about it—it would be a sad situation if *you* could convince only 30 percent of other humans that you were real! And so far there has only been one program that surmounted this bar, a chatbot called "Eugene Goostman," which fooled 33 percent of the judges at a 2014 Royal Society conference into believing that it was a thirteen-year-old Ukrainian boy.[6] The main way it did this was by making creative and somewhat random replies to questions and imitating an irreverent and impatient teenager.

But still, there was nobody in there—there was no feeling of being Eugene Goostman, no teenage boy—there was just a set of rules for generating responses. Goostman was reminiscent of the famous "Chinese room" thought experiment proposed by the philosopher John Searle. Searle wanted to show that computers can never be conscious—they can only follow instructions in a mechanical way. He illustrated this with the example of a person who is locked in a room with a set of instructions for translating Chinese symbols into a different set of Chinese symbols, just according to their shapes. As Searle pointed out, even if this person were able to properly translate the Chinese words, that wouldn't mean they understood Chinese.[7] What would it take for a computer to make the leap from mere instruction-following to true understanding? For Goostman to be "real"?

Let's take a fictional example. Consider the character Data in the well-known TV show *Star Trek: The Next Generation*.[8] Data is an android run by computer software. But he wants to be a real human being. He is insecure about his own existential status and is trying to confirm it somehow. In this sense, Data is like us. We aren't sure that we have real effects in the world (which is only what the determinists tell us)—that is, we aren't sure that our sense of being selves-in-charge isn't a delusion. And neither is Data.

I'd suggest that this is precisely the feature that best signals a "real" human being—that the entity is emotionally involved in the existential dilemmas of consciousness, freedom, and death. When the entity seems to be aware of these kinds of issues (as is Data), we are more likely to think that entity is a real person. We sense the depths at play, that there is an actual (in addition to a merely simulated) human being down in there. Thus, paradoxically, insecurity may be the very thing that signals to others that there is something deep and real within us—as suggested by philosopher Alan Watts in his 1951 book *The Wisdom of Insecurity*—or, as I would suggest, in an AI.[9] Perhaps to be fully human is to be aware that we are finite, and that there are depths within ourselves that our conscious minds cannot grasp.

A promising way to think about simulated personality may be to consider the four functions of the symbolic self. Does the character Data interact with others in a way that requires him to create a face, with which to interface with other faces (the first function of the symbolic self)? Viewers of the show know that he does just this, and very likably. He seems authentic. Does he try to defend his self-conception, and to protect it from being invalidated (the second function)? Apparently so—it matters to Data that he be treated like any other human crew member rather than as a mere computer program. Does he use his thoughts and self-perceptions to decide what to do, what goals to pursue (the third function)? Evidently so—after all, he is the chief science officer aboard the USS *Enterprise*, helping to decide what the ship will do next. Does he try to represent his own underlying mental state, within his consciousness (the fourth function of the symbolic self)? Yes, he reflects on his thoughts and perceptions, trying to understand what they might mean and what they are telling him. Is Data concerned with existential issues more broadly? Yes. Several episodes of the show explore Data's personal dilemmas and the current existential quandaries in which he finds himself.

These reflections suggest that AI researchers won't succeed in creating convincing artificial personalities until those personalities have a symbolic self, with all that implies. There needs to be a powerful executive process that can run things, but that is missing information and thus isn't sure where to go; there must be attempts to situate the current moment within a broader story that encompasses the history of the entity, attempts to confirm and extend the reality of the subjective agent, and attempts to access deeper patterns and potentials of which the subjective agent is currently unaware. In other words, there should be both an unconscious level to the artificial personality, which can supply insights and input, but in subtle ways; and a conscious level to the personality, which is able to call forth, but also able to ignore, those insights. An effective artificial personality should have both system 1 processes (automatic, habitual, intuitive) and system 2 processes (conscious, intentional, rational) going on within it.

Maybe the most important thing that a convincing artificial personality would need to have is the ability to care. That is, it would have emotions—it would feel disappointed if things turned out differently than it intended, and joyful if it managed to get what it wanted. But what does it mean to feel? Emotion research is a huge field, which I won't even try to canvass. But bodily responses are a critical component of emotions. When we humans feel an emotion, our bodies express and show it: our heart rates increase, our pupils flare, and our breathing speeds up. The faces of the later-to-be-convicted pedophile priests already showed that they were living in a compromised way. Perhaps, without bodies, AIs will never be able to have emotions—and thus may never be able to become truly sentient. They may never be able to care.

One way to solve this problem might be to install AIs directly into the body/brain system of a person. In the future, advances in the (not-yet-existent) field of personality engineering might give us inner mental companions that are AIs. Perhaps these companions could be spliced into the brains of the children of the future in such a way that the AIs directly perceive the minds and experiences of their hosts—their thoughts and feelings, their pains and pleasures. Such inner companions might be able to talk to their people by stimulating language areas of the brain. They could serve as wise teachers, giving children lessons and helping them to develop their minds as they grow. They might also serve as trustworthy companions, who are sympathetic and understanding, but at the same time can provide a valuable external perspective from outside a person's own thought processes. Remember, the ability to call forth a "generalized other" in one's mind has long been thought to be critical for cognitive development. In this case, the generalized-other perspective wouldn't come from our imaginations; instead, it would come from a computer program that would teach us how to do it.

Most intriguingly, perhaps these embedded AI companions could use the lifetime of data they collect about their humans to develop increasingly accurate models of unique human personalities via machine learning. Over time they would get better and better at predicting what people would do next, approaching unprecedented levels of accuracy. Imagine a digital assistant that told you, every morning, what you would do that day, given your current life-configuration. Would you want to go along with those predictions, or confound and disprove them?

I have said that one way we know that humans have free will is that science will never be able to fully predict what we will do in advance. Here, I somewhat take that back: devices using machine learning could perhaps predict people's behavior with a very high (but probably never perfect) degree of accuracy. This is especially the case if the machine had huge amounts of relevant data—including not just what a given individual had actually done in all past situations of their lives, but also what they had thought and felt prior to making their decisions within those situations.

If our dedicated AI was able to use such data to accurately predict what each of us would do before we did it, would this mean that we didn't have free will? Again, human unpredictability is one of the pillars of my argument for free will. If an AI can accurately predict our behavior, are we predetermined after all?

Not so fast! One of the main problems with machine learning is that the computer scientists who create the programs typically have no idea how they reach their conclusions. The program is a "black box," using far more information than a human brain can handle in ways that a human brain can't understand.[10]

In psychology research, we still try to develop theoretical explanations of psychological processes. Then we use those explanations to generate hypotheses, which we test by collecting relevant data (the deductive approach). We often find support for our explanations (they are better than nothing), but overall, they fall well short. In fact, this was the old way that AI research was conducted: researchers made assumptions about how people thought and then tried to implement those assumptions in computer architecture. In the new wave of AI, in machine learning, the AI is turned loose to find its own way to the answers, through *induction*. Nobody knows what the machine is really doing—what patterns it is learning and what information it is using to make its predictions.

So maybe our conclusions about free will remain the same: if no human scientist can use their own understanding to predict what AI models of people will do (just as they can't predict what the people themselves will do), then maybe people remain free (for now, at least). AI researchers are trying hard to figure out how to explain what AI models are doing—to go beyond just observing their outputs to understanding those outputs, and understanding how the computer arrived at them. Maybe these efforts will work in the end. Or maybe AI researchers are just rediscovering the same problem that has long plagued psychologists: the problem that human behavior is massively complex, such that our attempts to cast a prespecified explanatory web over behavior are always incomplete. I suspect that the latter is the case.

Let's talk a little more about the idea of a computed companion lodged within our own minds, one that can talk to us while trying to develop an increasingly accurate statistical model of our minds. In the future, human beings will presumably still die; their bodies will wear out, and the brain-based selves that they have constructed will die with them. But perhaps their experiences and perspectives won't be lost to the world as they are now—because AIs will be able to continue to run their (now highly elaborated) prediction models of their humans after the death of those humans, applying that model to perceive itself and make choices. A model could even speak with its human's voice, based on its conclusions and decisions about what that human would have said. In other words, maybe the computer model will be able to take over after a person is gone and continue that person's existence in the world.

If so, would that model still *be* that person? Maybe so—after all, the AI model thinks almost exactly like the original person did. So, given the same input, it should react the same way. Also, the AI knows the person far more intimately than anybody else did, perhaps even more intimately than the person knew himself or herself. So even though the "wet" brain, which was based on the activity of neurons, is gone, maybe the surviving AI, based on the activity of "dry" silicon chips, could *be* the person? Or maybe not. On further reflection, maybe the AI is still only a clever imitation of the person, a computerized fake.

Such questions of identity are quite old in the field of philosophy of mind. If every board and timber within a wooden ship is replaced bit by bit, is it still the same ship at the end? This is the "Ship of Theseus" question, first proposed by the Greek philosopher Plutarch.[11] Our first response might be to say no. But then we might have to say the same thing about ourselves, because nearly all of our cells are replaced during our lifetimes by new cells. In fact, 98 percent of our atoms are replaced every year.

Despite this, we still remember ourselves as children— we remember our life stories and the changes we have been through. So maybe the main thing that makes us "us" is the continuing narrative that we live in, the evolving story that we tell about ourselves. But if that is true, then maybe a computer model of us, which also "knows" that story and continues to live it, could be us.

Assuming that such AIs cared about things—that they had a true emotional inside—they would doubtless face some serious existential dilemmas. It is likely that a surviving AI would want to believe that it was the legitimate continuation of the original person. But one reason the AI might remain unsure of this is that the AI would run on silicon instead of, essentially, meat. There might be lingering chauvinism within future societies, a sort of "meat privilege," which holds that intelligent entities only deserve full respect and citizenship if they were born into a biological body. Another reason the surviving AI might remain existentially uncertain about its identity is that its own story would continue to evolve after its human's death, perhaps in ways that the human's story could not have evolved. It is one thing to merely continue the person's story and mode of living; it is another to radically depart from that story and mode of living, as would likely happen in some cases.

For example, what if the surviving AI became a champion for the rights of artificial intelligences, a position that the original person never would have taken? Only after the original person's death, after finding out what it is like to be a second-class (merely digital) citizen, might the surviving AI be ready to make such a radical shift in attitude. Its way of thinking might become very different from that of its original human, such that its symbolic self would change.

*   *   *

I've briefly touched on some of the critical issues that designers of artificial personalities will face. I've suggested that the best way to make such personalities seem real (so they can pass the Turing test), and perhaps even to *be* real (in the same way humans are real), is to set up conditions for them to develop a symbolic self: the sense of being the choosing executive within a mind, one that can only "think slow" and that does not have direct access to the faster processes going on down in the machinery. Paradoxically, by separating the artificial self from itself and giving it executive powers that it must use, but without full information, and by giving it the desire and capacity to know itself better, and the desire to persuade other selves that it is real and legitimate—by giving it insecurity, like that felt by Data—we can perhaps cross the boundary between the living and the mechanical, to create animators of the mechanical who are just as sentient as we are. It would be interesting to get to know them!

CHAPTER 10

THE CREATIVE PROCESS OF LIVING

Back when Amy was a college student, she volunteered for environmental causes, going door to door asking people to sign petitions and helping to organize her town's annual Earth Day celebration, where she talked to people and passed out information. In the process she formed close relationships with like-minded others, especially with another young woman, Marta, whose zeal and dedication she admired. Amy decided to go to law school, hoping to gain tools to continue working for the planet.

Armed with her idealistic motivation and her acute intelligence, Amy did very, very well in her law school program. She ended up in the top 5 percent of her class and was selected to help edit her school's law review journal, a high-status position only available to the best of the best. Amy enjoyed her success and the boosted self-esteem that came with it. She began to think of herself as a legal ace, somebody who could sort through and solve any legal problem. She also began to forget about the environmental goals that had brought her to law school in the first place. "Why pigeonhole myself?" she thought.

Upon graduation, Amy was courted by several large private law firms. She took the job that paid the most, even though it involved working for a firm that didn't do much environmental law (and when it did, it usually worked on the side of the polluters). Why did she take this job? Because that's what the top-down culture of her law school had taught her to do. The best students should seek the highest-status, highest-paying jobs possible—these students were the most attractive targets in a dating game, and they should get what they were worth. Amy told herself that once she gained her footing in her new profession, she would get back to the environment thing. But she never seemed to find the right time.

Amy isn't a real person but an amalgamation of many people I've encountered throughout my career, particularly in my research on lawyers and law students. The problem I've studied, though not exclusive to lawyers, is particularly acute among them. I got into this line of research after I met Larry Krieger, a Florida State University law professor, on a positive psychology listserv. Krieger has been engaged in a long-term effort to reform legal education in the United States, which he argues is deeply dehumanizing for students. The US legal education system forces students into fierce competition with each other. Professors typically grade on a curve so severe that even 90 percent mastery of the material might equate to a grade of only a C or even a D. Law-school culture often teaches students to ignore their own feelings and values and instead uncritically adopt the client's agenda as a "hired gun." Much class time is based on the Socratic method, in which students are called upon to think aloud. During these interchanges, professors sometimes publicly humiliate the student. As a result, as research going back to the 1980s has shown, students' sense of well-being plummets.[1] In a sense, students are "brainwashed." Many of them lose touch with who they were when they started and buy into an extrinsic value system of competition, status, and affluence. This value system does not serve them well.

In our first jointly authored study, published in 2004, Krieger and I followed a sample of law students across all three years of law school.[2] We found that students' intrinsic motivation for studying the law dramatically decreased during the first year. This was similar to what happened for the Pacific Crest Trail through-hikers, but there the similarity stopped. Rather than developing stronger identified motivation to compensate for the hardships, like the through-hikers, law students experienced a decline in identified motivation as well. Their confidence in the value and importance of what they were learning faded. As their intrinsic and identified motivations waned, external motivation was left to do the heavy lifting alone—a classic undermining effect. And consistent with other findings about the correlation between decreases in intrinsic motivation and decreases in mental health, not only did our sampling of students report a lower sense of well-being, but a number of them also reached clinical or near-clinical levels of depression.

Krieger and I also found a very interesting dynamic at play: students who began law school with the highest levels of intrinsic motivation—people like our fictional Amy—tended to attain the highest grades during their first year. They rose to the challenge of mastering very complex material, making that material their own. But then, many of these top students became corrupted by their success. We measured students' career aspirations twice over the first year of law school, once in September and again the following May. We focused on the distinction between "money" jobs (high pay, high status, more competition) and "service" jobs (lower pay, lower status, less competition). It turned out that the students receiving the highest first-year grades typically shifted *away* from wanting to use the law to help others or serve causes and shifted *toward* wanting to make as much money as possible. They also shifted in their extrinsic versus intrinsic goal profiles, becoming more interested in looking good, and less interested in serving their communities. People like Amy forgot who they were and what was important to them.

Fast-forward twenty years. Let's say that by her mid-forties, Amy has become a partner in a big-city law firm, one that often helps companies to circumvent environmental regulations. She is working more than sixty hours a week, and she is raking in a very large salary—far more money than she has time to spend. Unfortunately, she is also miserable, but she doesn't know why. She hates her life, and she struggles with alcoholism. She goes through serial short-term relationships, in which she is often emotionally abused by her partner. It seems that at some level she wants to be punished; she thinks she deserves to suffer.

If you asked forty-something Amy about her main goal in life, her answer would be, "Hold on for ten more years, to get the biggest payoff." She would be willing to spend another decade in misery before she quit the job she hated, just so she could have stacks of money in hand. Amy's family might be distressed at the changes they saw in her: What happened to the happy and idealistic young woman they knew? Could anything arrest the downward spiral Amy seemed stuck in? Could she somehow "grow her way out of her problems"? How does personal growth happen, anyway?

Recently, my research has explored the striking similarity between how people grow and how they create. The most famous model of the creative process was proposed by Graham Wallas in 1926.[3] Wallas's four-stage model is still highly relevant within creativity research today.[4] It says that creativity begins when someone makes a conscious attempt to find an answer to an artistic, scientific, or other problem that seems, intuitively, to have a solution—even though the person cannot yet see it. During this preparation phase, the conscious mind (system 2) works on defining the problem for the nonconscious mind (system 1), thus calling upon that mind for work.

Typically, creators don't find the answers to such questions right away: they may even give up in frustration and do something else. But the second stage of the process has nevertheless begun: incubation. During this stage the nonconscious mind continues to work, making connections and responding to hints, cues, and clues, all without the person's awareness. Next, if this process works, comes the insight stage, when the "aha!" moment occurs. The creator has a sudden revelation and consciously recognizes a potential or possibility that had not appeared before or that they had overlooked. At that moment, the person feels that the answer has been found, or is at least within reach. Last comes the verification and elaboration stage, in which the creator thinks carefully about the implications of the discovery, follows it through, and confirms that it really is the answer that was sought.

Recent research I've done with students Ryan Goffredi and Liudmilla Titova showed that the process of recognizing what we really want—out of a career, out of a life—follows a very similar sequence of steps. We may feel stuck—we know there is something more for us in life, something we are not seeing. But try as we might, we don't know what it is yet (preparation). We may even give up looking, possibly for long periods of time (incubation). But our questions and reflections continue to exert influence beneath the surface. If the process is successful, we arrive at the "aha!" moment (insight) when the clouds part and the sun comes out. But we must be open to that moment, and afterward, we must have the courage to follow our new insight to its logical conclusion (verification/elaboration).

This model applies very well to Amy's case. Suppose that after an intense conversation with her brother at a family gathering, Amy begins to think seriously about her misery. How can she be so successful and so unhappy at the same time? She knows something is wrong, but what? Is there a way out? Her unhappiness makes it difficult for her to see other possibilities—she feels trapped and thinks she will always be unhappy. At least Amy has begun asking herself new questions. She has entered the preparation stage of the creative growth process.

Nothing much seems to happen for quite some time—Amy is in the incubation stage. One morning, while sitting at her desk, the thought of her old friend Marta comes to mind, seemingly unbidden. Amy hasn't thought about Marta in at least fifteen years; they have completely lost touch with each other. Why did the thought come up then? Amy feels a spark of interest in the thought but quickly forgets about it in the press of her day. Another three weeks go by. Then the thought of Marta appears again. Is deeper Amy trying to tell surface Amy something? Again, surface Amy quickly forgets about it. When the thought appears for the third time, Amy *notices*. "Whatever happened to her?" she wonders. She does a quick Google search. Lo and behold, it turns out that Marta has parlayed her degree in environmental science into a very relevant career. Marta has her own consulting company, advising clients on how to reduce their ecological footprints and operate more sustainably. She also helps clients prepare lawsuits to stop polluters.

Amy is interested in this revelation, but that's as far as it goes for several months. A couple of times during this period Amy considers reaching out to Marta, but she feels ashamed of who she has become: she doesn't want to risk Marta's disapproval or contempt. Despite her great success in the legal world and her high salary, Amy feels like a hollow shell, a person that nobody with any integrity would want to know.

So Amy continues spiraling down, even spending two weeks in alcohol rehab. This helps for a while, but soon she's back to where she was before. Why? Because the central problem of her life remains unrecognized and unsolved.

One weekend, Amy hits rock bottom. She even thinks of taking her own life and begins writing her will. But, once again, the thought of her old friend Marta comes to mind. This time she seizes it, recognizing it for what it is: a cue to a new way of life. Amy's executive function now goes to work. She composes and sends an email to Marta, congratulating her on her success in the field in which they had once shared a common interest. The email is rather apologetic: Amy feels ashamed of who she has become and sheepish about reaching out.

What happens next is very encouraging. Marta is glad to hear from Amy and sorry that Amy is dissatisfied with her job. Marta doesn't condemn Amy; instead, she is supportive and understanding. Marta even mentions the possibility of Amy coming to work for Marta's company. She needs a lawyer skilled in the intricacies of environmental law, even if that person has usually tried to help companies skirt that law. In fact, that is what Marta needs most: a lawyer who knows all the tricks, after all, is best positioned to defeat those tricks. Would Amy consider interviewing for the position?

Part of Amy is very intrigued by this idea, but another part of her is frightened. If she takes the job, she will make less than half of what she is currently making and will have to move to a new city. What will her current colleagues say about such a decision? Will they call her crazy? Despite her misery, Amy is still quite attached to the idea of herself as an elite lawyer working for a prestigious firm—she has ascended to the very top of her profession. Can she really give that up to take a job that her peers will consider a step down?

In Amy's dilemma we can see all four functions of the symbolic self, but we can also see considerable conflict between these functions. Recall that one important job of the symbolic self is to represent the self to other selves, to project a praiseworthy face to the other faces in the environment, to manage the interface between the personality and other personalities within the grand hierarchy. Amy was worried about what her current peers would think and say about her. Would they think she was a loser if she threw away her elite partnership to become an underpaid tree hugger? But at the same time, Amy was afraid of what her friend Marta thought of her—perhaps as a sellout to corporate greed. It seemed impossible to reconcile these two external faces.

Another important job of the symbolic self is to defend its own current structure—to protect who we think we are. In this case, Amy was afraid to let go of the self-image she had cultivated over a period of twenty years as an elite lawyer who could maximize her clients' financial return. Although there are many similarities between the growth process and the creative process, they are also different in an important way. Usually, creators and researchers aren't afraid of what they might find out, and they aren't afraid to go beyond the status quo. That's what they want! They are "riding the positive feedback train" to a new discovery. When the creative accomplishment involves recasting one's very identity into a new form, however, a person may have to push through considerable internal resistance. As Amy discovered, it takes courage and boldness to overcome the defensive functioning of the symbolic self.

That's why the thought of Marta had to recur several times before Amy was willing to follow the lead.

Also recall the fourth function of the symbolic self: to represent the totality of the personality as accurately as possible. This means that the story the symbolic self lives in should be one that allows the person's deeper dispositions and interests, down in system 1, to be expressed. If the symbolic self consistently fails in this regard, then it remains in danger of being overthrown or supplanted—because it isn't doing its job. It isn't helping the person to adapt and thrive. This was certainly the case for Amy, whose image of herself as an elite legal ace was getting quite wobbly.

To follow up with Amy's story, though, let's say that one morning, after a run, Amy finds that everything has shifted around in her mind. She realizes that she took a wrong turn long ago—and that this detour has taken her away from herself, even to the point of suicide. In thinking about Marta's offer, Amy now recognizes it for the rare opportunity it is: the chance to start again, to return to her youthful ideals, to begin moving down a more fulfilling path. She also sees her current high-power, high-paying job in a new light—as a terrible misuse of her precious time, something she could barely tolerate for another week, much less ten more years. Amy accepts Marta's offer, and immediately things begin changing for the better in her life.

Fast-forward once again: On Amy's sixty-second birthday, she thinks back on her career. She has been working with Marta's company for sixteen years (as a partner for the past ten) and has never regretted making the jump. Where she once relied on extrinsic and self-pressured motivation to push through each day of work, she now has intrinsic and identified motivation—the sense of enjoying what she is doing, and of finding it meaningful even when it gets to be a grind. And where she was once miserable, she now feels happy and fulfilled—she is contributing to the world in a way that expresses her deepest values and beliefs in her daily life. Most important: she never wants to retire! Work is so interesting and rewarding: Why would she ever want to stop?

Amy has piled up much less money in the past sixteen years than she would have accumulated if she had stayed in her old job. But so what? Maybe doing what we want is more important than doing what makes us money. Happiness research shows this to be unequivocally true: the correlation between autonomous work motivation and subjective well-being is much stronger than the correlation between income and subjective well-being.[5] Furthermore, beyond about $90,000, increasing personal income makes little difference in predicting SWB.[6] Enough is enough; after that, other things matter much more. In making their decisions, people often act as if the opposite were true—as if money were the main thing, always. But once again, our "affective forecasts," our predictions about how our current choices will affect our later well-being, can be way off base. We can be so clueless up in our mental worlds!

Krieger and I demonstrated this paradox in a very concrete way in a 2014 study. We gave a survey to members of four US state bar associations, then compared 1,145 service job lawyers (working in government agencies, as public defenders, in private practice or small family firms, and the like) to 1,414 money job lawyers (in litigation, securities, finance, and so on).[7] Although we found that money job lawyers really did make more money than service job lawyers ($90,000 a year more, on average), we also found that money job lawyers were less happy and felt less fulfilled than service job lawyers. They were also heavier drinkers. Although their higher income supplied a small boost for their sense of well-being, that boost was more than wiped out by the much larger negative effects of doing a job they hated. This left them with a net disadvantage in their happiness levels compared to the service job lawyers. According to typical law-school culture, it is the service job lawyers who were the "losers" in the competition. Our study suggests otherwise.

Amy's inspirational voyage of self-discovery may sound familiar—after all, it is the template for many novels, plays, and films where a character is initially misguided about something they are choosing to do. Like Charles Dickens's Scrooge, they don't know what is important in the first part of the story, and they need to learn some life lessons. In many such stories, the character begins questing for something different, and begins asking "What's wrong?" and "Is this all there is?" (preparation). Many of them also involve a long hiatus (incubation) following this questioning period, followed by a sudden insight when the character suddenly sees, through the mists, a direction forward (illumination). This same thing can easily happen in real life: we have an organismic valuing process that is always capable of supplying us with valuable insights if we can just recognize what it is telling us and find the courage to follow where it leads, as Amy finally did (elaboration).

~~~

Amy spent decades in misery, reaching some very low lows, before she took the initiative to email Marta and set her growth spiral in motion. How can we learn to live well now, so that we don't end up throwing away decades of our lives in pursuit of the wrong things?

One key is recognizing when we are unhappy and starting to ask questions. Emotions are signals that tell us how we are doing. When Amy finally recognized the signals, she started asking herself the right questions. This questioning set things into motion, so she could begin to escape from her self-imposed prison.

A second key for good living is as simple as this: *once you have an idea what you want, set goals.* Goal-setting is the primary superpower of the symbolic self living up in the verbal world: the power to articulate aspirations and intentions. As the acting executives within our brain's highest-level control system (the default mode network), as the directors of our minds and bodies, we can say: "I want X." This capacity opens up a world of possibilities to us, whether it is helping the environment, writing a novel, or deepening a friendship. Once we've articulated goals, we can make plans for how to go about achieving them. Then we can start trying to reduce the discrepancy between where we are now and where we would like to be. Recognizing such aspirations can begin to nudge us in a new direction even if we don't succeed right away.

Indeed, merely stating our goals aloud can have huge ramifications. I often tell students, "Just say it. Just say what you want to happen." Simply stating intentions activates us. It lets us "cross the Rubicon" from deliberation to implementation, thereby gaining the help of many automatic mental mechanisms. These mechanisms are there to protect and support our stated intentions and help us get what we've said we want. Articulating our goals, way up in system 2, puts many nonconscious processes to work for us down in system 1. Try it!

Getting what we want can still be very difficult. We may not realize (at least at first) what it will take to reach our goal—and we may not want it badly enough (yet), and may suffer failures, or become discouraged. But in the process, we can learn, and learn to do better the next time. In the words of the musician Jimmy Cliff, "You can get it if you really want—but you must try, try and try, try and try—you'll succeed at last." The main thing is not to confuse difficulty with impossibility. Don't accept that your behavior is irrevocably controlled by the situation just because the situation is frustrating. This is one of the many problems with the doctrine of determinism—that accepting it tempts people to give up prematurely, inviting a sense of stuckness. In the midst of a setback, we can very easily overgeneralize and take on a sense of learned helplessness.[8]

At the same time, it's important to recognize that our difficulties are sometimes due to wanting the *wrong things* and setting the wrong goals. Living in a verbal world (system 2) that is not the same as our entire mind and organism, we are free to choose poorly—going after the goals our parents or friends suggest to us, or that the larger society seems to promote, rather than listening to the signals from deeper in our minds and bodies that might steer us in a different direction and give us the motivation we need to move forward.

"Choosing poorly" is exactly what Amy did in the first part of her career. But life is an experiment, and she eventually got it right.

So how can we learn what to want—learn how to select goals that will keep us going in the long term, that will inspire us enough to surmount anything, that can and will fulfill us?

We've already seen several ways to give ourselves a leg up in selecting the right goals—goals that are concordant with our deepest desires. The most basic technique is to ask yourself why you *might* want to do X before you pick it. Is it because X is an intriguing and fascinating topic, and because doing X sounds challenging and enjoyable to you? If so, you have intrinsic motivation to do X (first discussed in Chapter 4). When we are intrinsically motivated, we are often in what psychologists call *flow*: fully engaged, operating at the current limits of our knowledge and skill, learning rapidly and enjoying ourselves.[9]

Not every healthy or meaningful activity can be enjoyable. So also ask yourself, "Would doing X be an expression of my heartfelt values and commitments, such that X continues to seem important even when doing X becomes boring or difficult?" If so, you have identified motivation—the second major form of autonomous motivation—to do X. If you have both intrinsic and identified motivation, then you are on the right track. Your verbal mind (system 2) has managed to identify a self-concordant avenue of behavior, one that is well aligned with your deeper personality. Go for it, even if the way forward is uncertain. The Pacific Crest Trail hikers who developed more identified motivation were both more likely to finish the trail and more likely to derive happiness benefits from the accomplishment than the hikers for whom identified motivation was not as strong.

In considering whether to accept Marta's offer, Amy applied this very technique: before making a move, she considered her motivations for pursuing the new career direction. She concluded that she would enjoy the challenges presented by the new job (intrinsic motivation), and that she would benefit from returning to her long-suppressed environmental values (identified motivation). Her prestigious law firm job, by contrast, was neither intellectually stimulating nor aligned with her deeper values. Recognizing this made Amy more confident that taking the new position was the right choice.

On the other hand, if your reason for selecting a particular goal is that you "ought to" do it, even though you don't really want to—beware. This is a sign that your executive function has been infiltrated by an alien impulse, one that it can't fully take in and "swallow," or internalize. This type of "ought to" feeling is introjected motivation, in which one part of the self tries to force another part to do something. Introjected motivation is not entirely negative, because it represents at least partial internalization. It can be effective, and sometimes it is necessary—whether it's getting us to take out the trash or to finish some project that we started. The PCT through-hikers who developed stronger introjected motivation were more likely to complete the trail, just like those who developed stronger identified motivation. Nevertheless, for the introjected hikers, finishing was more of a relief than a genuine triumph.

And finally, if your reason for selecting a goal is that you think you *have* to, even though you don't *want* to, this is external motivation. Again, beware. Yes, there are many things we must do in life, and external motivation, like introjected motivation, can help us get them done. I have to register my car next week, which involves first doing several annoying chores, then standing in a long line at the state office. I wouldn't be doing it if it weren't for the external motivation of not wanting to pay a fine! Many things in life work this way. But when it comes to selecting major life-goals that will guide you for decades, a feeling of "having" to do X is a sign that you might be choosing wrongly. Keep looking and thinking, and see if the feeling changes—can you at least begin to internalize the idea of doing X, so that it begins to feel more like an expression of your own will?

Let's take a concrete example. A sixty-year-old man might start out thinking he *has* to quit his job to take care of his aging mother (external motivation). It has become clear that she can no longer live independently. But with some inner work and reflection, he may discover that part of him kind of wants to do it: Mom has little time left, and he probably owes it to her— he "should" do it. This would be introjected motivation and would be a good start. And maybe, over time, he can even develop fully identified motivation for taking care of her— perhaps by recognizing a rich opportunity to create new meaning and closure in their relationship. This may well happen, because, as I've found in my research, the internalization process tends to operate automatically over time. Of course, we can't (or shouldn't) *always* internalize what we find ourselves doing; sometimes our own resistance is a signal that we need to try something else. So the man might also legitimately decide to get professional care for his mother, so that he can continue working in his fulfilling job. Every case is different, and admittedly, such judgments can be very difficult to make.

What should we do when we're not sure about our motivation, or when we must choose between two equally attractive (or equally unattractive) options? Another strategy is to choose the goal or activity that is most eudaimonic: the one that reflects the best within us by expressing our inherent desires to connect and create, to grow and develop, to be nobler and better people. According to Aristotle, eudaimonic living involves the pursuit of excellence and virtue. Virtues come in a lot of different forms, but they all involve three main factors: our ethical sense, and desire to be guided by a moral compass; our social sense, and desire to help others and go deeper with them; and our intellectual sense, and desire to better understand and comprehend the world. Although eudaimonia is a very broad category, and can be hard to pin down, we can still know when we are behaving in eudaimonic ways. At these times, we experience deep satisfaction. If something is meaningful and challenging, and if it brings you satisfaction and a sense of well-being, then you know you are on the right track. For Amy, the transition to Marta's company fulfilled her desire for "excellent activity in accordance with the soul," which is one of Aristotle's descriptions of eudaimonia.

Amy's story also reveals the important role that time can play in our decision-making process. As we've seen, over time, people tend to shift toward more intrinsic and satisfying goals and away from extrinsic and less satisfying goals. Our non-conscious minds can know what to want even when we don't, and if we keep listening, they can push us in self-beneficial directions. Eventually Amy's organismic valuing process broke through, alerting her to a more fulfilling possibility for her life.

But what if waiting isn't possible, or if, like Amy, we feel miserable? Sometimes we must do more than just wait. We can *ask* ourselves for help. As the conscious executive within our minds, we can request information from our nonconscious minds. We constantly do this with our everyday decisions ("What do I feel like wearing today? Hmm...green feels cheery"), but we can also learn to do it with larger tasks ("What is the best route to the life I really want? Hmm...this degree program feels right!"). And we need to be able to hear and accept the answers when they come. It took Amy a long while to start asking herself questions, and then it took more time to start hearing, and finally acting upon, the answers she received.

Researcher Marcia Baxter Magolda's excellent 2009 book, *Authoring Your Life*, provides many fascinating examples of people learning to call forth their inner wisdom and then taking it seriously.[10] In one longitudinal study of adult development, she found that "participants had to actively work on listening to their new and fragile inner voices." The good news is that participants knew that this work was important and were willing to do that work. "Through effort I have learned what I value and am trying to grow in ways that will embody those values," one participant told her. Another said, "I am learning to hear my own voice, behind the clutter of the external world." We occupants of system 2 can learn to activate system 1, and to get it to do work for us.

According to Baxter Magolda, being open to the new is the most difficult part of the growth process. It requires us to overcome outdated or incorrect beliefs about who we are and what we are capable of doing—our attachment to a limited view of ourselves. Recall that one of the three functions of the symbolic self, according to Constantine Sedikides and John Skowronski, was to defend the structure of that self. This is important—we need to protect ourselves from the disempowering judgments of others, or else we'll be miserable and easily bullied.

*   *   *

But the defensive function of our symbolic selves can stand in the way of our growth and development. Sometimes the old self-image (like Amy's "legal ace" identity) isn't worth defending. When that is the case we need to let go of our outdated self-concepts ("me's") and start trusting the deeper parts of ourselves that are trying to be heard ("I's"). If we can be smart enough to ask ourselves the right questions, mindful enough to listen to the answers, and then brave enough to follow through, we can steer our ship of self into uncharted new waters, where joy and fulfillment await. This is the promise of resolving to be freely determined—even if it sometimes brings pain.

EPILOGUE

LIVING WELL TOGETHER

As a young man I received a fortune cookie that both amused and disturbed me: "A change for the better will be made against you." It was probably a typo or mistranslation, but it sounded ominous. And it raises an important question about free will that we have yet to answer. In this book, I've mostly focused on the functions and capacities of the symbolic self, the psychological entity that we each believe ourselves to be. The symbolic self gives us a way to listen to the unconscious signals arising from lower levels in the grand hierarchy, to use that information to select specific goals, and then to coordinate the activity of our minds and bodies to try to reach them.

But this is a rather individualistic focus. What about our *relationships*—our mentors, leaders, teachers, partners, parents, and friends? In Chapter 2 we saw that the grand hierarchy continues on up, far beyond our own bodies, to include many other bodies, ranging from one other person to families and other groups, including teams and other organizations, and finally to entire cultures spread far and wide. What happens when my change for the better is your change for the worse? In other words, how can we, as free agents, best relate to other free agents whose interests we may not always share?

First, it's critical for us to connect our stories to the stories of other people, and to feel known and appreciated by them and vice versa. And we're more likely to get along with others—and even get them to do what we want!—when we support their autonomy, rather than trying to control them—especially when we are in positions of power and status. We should try to be good stewards of the social power invested in us. But how might such practices take us beyond our everyday sense of self and mode of operating with others? What is different in such cases?

One hint is provided by Constantine Sedikides and John Skowronski's idea that the symbolic self is a third-order form of awareness. All animals are presumed to have first-order awareness, meaning that they can distinguish between themselves and the world. Other brainy social species besides ourselves, such as apes and dolphins, have second-order awareness as well—an understanding of the self as an object with certain characteristics. But as far as we know, only humans have third-order awareness: we understand ourselves as complex and persisting characters in a very long dramatic play. The capacity to construct symbolic selves evolved because it provides people with ways to manage and imagine personally important events—ways to steer themselves toward more adaptive or fulfilling outcomes.

Sedikides and Skowronski's three-level scheme raises a fascinating question: Could there be there a *fourth*-order type of awareness, one that transcends the first three? Perhaps this would be some sort of "next step" in the evolution of consciousness. Based on the emergentist logic of the grand hierarchy, it's a reasonable question. But what might this fourth-order awareness be like? How might it reach beyond the third-order awareness of the symbolic self? In short, what would fourth-order awareness contain or be about?

Here is one stab at an answer: In third-order awareness, we are each characters in a drama taking place within our own minds, and our characters are separate from every other character. And, objectively speaking, our symbolic selves *do* exist in complete "existential isolation" from each other, because we have no direct way to contact another person's brain, no way to know directly what another person is experiencing. Even our closest loved ones are always on the other side of an uncrossable gulf, whether we realize it or not. What's more, we ourselves are unknowable to anybody else.[1] Nobody else can know what it is like to be you, at this moment, or, after you die, what it was like to be you when you were living. When we are gone, we are gone forever.

And the kicker is, it's even hard for *us* to know what it's like to be us—for me to know what it's like to be me, or for you to know what it's like to be you! Because of the partially cut-off status of the symbolic self, and the restricted purview of the ego tunnel, we are radically free to *not* be ourselves. Remember Daniel Kahneman's odd statement: "The self who does my living is like a stranger to me." And remember Tim Wilson's book, aptly titled *Strangers to Ourselves*. Such an odd state of affairs!

Maybe we don't *need* to know exactly what others are experiencing, or even what we ourselves are experiencing, to make a valuable contribution to the greater whole to which we belong. Deep down within our bodies, particular cells don't have direct access to "what it's like" to be other cells; nor do organs know what it's like to be other organs. Chemicals don't know about each other, and mostly, even our own thoughts don't know about each other. Despite this, our whole bodily system mostly gets along with itself.

If we extend this logic to our symbolic selves, it suggests that when selves are functioning well, they enhance the functioning of the larger systems or social organisms to which they belong. This should be true in the same way that blood cells help the functioning of the larger body. But what are those larger systems or organisms that encompass the symbolic self? Based on the logic of the grand hierarchy, it seems that fourth-order awareness should involve identification of the self with amalgamations of selves, all contained within social groups, organizations, or networks: "I am we and we are me."

This is not a new idea—there is a whole research literature on social and group identities that we haven't considered. This research shows that group identities are very powerful—witness the intensely partisan politics existing in the world today. But it's important to note that despite our cherished group identities, we are still ultimately isolated from other human minds, and even from inaccessible parts of our own minds. We can't access these places directly; we can only imagine them. Perhaps it doesn't matter that we can't fully know others, or even fully know ourselves, as long as we are functioning well as a collective. That can be very satisfying. A rich fourth-order network of symbolic selves, all sharing a common purpose, may be the very condition that humanity needs to get to in order to survive. But how do we get to that point—a collective awareness, working for common purposes—with compassion and empathy, retaining our individuality and the autonomy of each person in the process?

Fourth-order awareness could also be thought of in terms of narratives and the authorship of narratives (as in Jonathan Adler's study of how psychotherapy patients became more the authors of their lives). In fourth-order awareness, we would feel ourselves to be more than a single character playing its own part within its own life-story. Perhaps, at this next level up, we are invested in *the drama itself*—as if we were not just characters in a novel, doing whatever the author said we would do, but also have an authorship role ourselves, creating the future together, and very much want the story to reach a satisfying ending. We would want that good ending even if we might suffer or die along the way ("A change for the better will be made against you"). From this viewpoint, instead of just trying to be a respectable symbolic self within the society of other (separate) selves, we should try to take responsibility for the entire drama—serving a bit like shamans or midwives, helping our communities to birth unpredictable and magical cultural productions, even at a cost to ourselves.

Looking around the world, it is obvious that there are many remarkable, inspiring, and altogether luminous beings among us who are doing just this: working tirelessly to protect the environment, to promote basic human rights, to

bend the arc of justice (as in Martin Luther King Jr.'s unfor-
gettable words). But too many of us fall into a different kind
of group identity or narrative: the kind that pits "us" against
"them," a "good we" versus a "bad they." This tendency to define ourselves in terms of favored in-groups versus disdained
out-groups likely evolved early in hominid history, back when
tribalism was a necessary and beneficial adaptation. In an
increasingly global world, this "us versus them" mechanism
has outlived its usefulness. Soon, it seems, it will be now or
never—time to pull together.

The grand hierarchy is designed to explain how increasingly complex organisms evolve and function in the universe.
Humans may be the most complex organisms to emerge so far,
though in some ways we may be too smart for our own good,
so smart that it makes us dumb. The grand hierarchy shows
us how much all life depends on every level of organization,
all the way down to atoms, in order to exist. Furthermore, all
the levels within us share a mutual common fate—from the
cells in our bodies to our brains and our very selves: together,
we live or we die. And the same is true of humans within society: if society goes down, it doesn't matter who goes down
first or second, because we will all go in the end. Sadly, with
radical polarization, raging pandemics, and uncontrollable
climate change, it seems that "going down" may well become
our common fate.

Yet I remain cautiously optimistic about human nature
and its potential to adapt.[2] Evolution has continually solved
the problems posed by prior limitations, by creating new com-
posite structures as needed. These structures have always

transcended what existed before, going from nonliving matter to single-cell life, multicellular organisms, and on to thinking organisms, symbolic selves, group identities, and national governments. If a collectivistic group-mind process is necessary to solve the problems we now face, so be it. Still, down at the (critical) level of personality, our symbolic selves are much more than the sums of their parts. They are capable of much more than either selfishness or subservience. Let's hope our future societies can become more capable, too, and much more than the sum of their parts.

ACKNOWLEDGMENTS

I'd like to thank the following people who read and commented on earlier versions or particular parts of this book: Mike Barrett, Emma Berry, John Donaldson, Bryan Haynes, Eric Henney, Noah Heringman, Tim Kasser, Christian List, Frank Martela, Richard Ryan, Todd Schachtman, Constantine Sedikides, and Dan Turban.

ACKNOWLEDGMENTS

NOTES

Introduction: Why Free Will Matters

1. Christian List, *Why Free Will Is Real* (Cambridge, MA: Harvard University Press, 2019). List's book cuts through many entrenched philosophical conundrums by taking a psychological rather than a philosophical perspective on the free-will question.

2. Gilbert Ryle, *The Concept of Mind* (Chicago: University of Chicago Press, 1949). Ryle criticizes mind-body dualism of the type implied by Descartes, which is considered in the next paragraph.

3. Roger Penrose, *The Emperor's New Mind: Concerning Computers, Minds, and the Laws of Physics* (Oxford: Oxford University Press, 1989). In this book, Penrose, a Nobel Prize–winning physicist, outlines his quantum theory of consciousness, which says that consciousness has a critical transcendent role in the universe, simply by what it focuses attention on. Conscious perceptions "collapse the wave function" of quantum indeterminacy to produce specific events. Penrose's theory is bold, but not widely accepted.

4. See Kennon M. Sheldon, *Optimal Human Being: An Integrated Multi-Level Perspective* (Mahwah, NJ: Erlbaum, 2004). Although it was more technical than the present book, *Optimal Human Being* foreshadowed many of the same concepts. It omitted some key ideas and findings, however, that came in later years.

5. Roy Baumeister, "Free Will in Scientific Psychology," *Perspectives on Psychological Science* 3, no. 1 (2008): 14–19. This important review article focuses on self-control and rational choice as apparent evolved capacities of human beings.

6. Jean-Paul Sartre, *Being and Nothingness: An Essay on Phenomenological Ontology* (New York: Washington Square Press, 1969). Sartre said that "existence precedes essence." This means that we have no essential nature beyond that which we create for ourselves—self-creation is the essence of human nature, and choice is inescapable.

7. Viktor Frankl, *Man's Search for Meaning* (Vienna: Verlag für Jugend und Volk, 1946). Frankl analyzes how prisoners within Nazi camps responded to their terrible predicament, showing that maintaining a sense of purpose was crucial for survival.

Chapter 1: The Problems with Determinism

1. Sam Harris, *Free Will* (New York: Free Press, 2012). Harris argues for determinism primarily with reference to brain processes occurring beneath awareness.

2. John Horgan emphasized this point in his review of Sam Harris's book *Free Will*: "Will This Post Make Sam Harris Change His Mind About Free Will?," *Scientific American, Cross-Check* (blog), April 9, 2012, https://blogs.scientificamerican.com/cross-check/will-this-post-make-sam-harris-change-his-mind-about-free-will.

3. Richard Dawkins, *The Blind Watchmaker* (London: Penguin, 1986). Here Dawkins argues that complexity can emerge in the universe without a Divine Designer, and I agree. However, he also argues that human designers are equally superfluous in science, and here I do not agree. Human designers are largely running the show, although not necessarily well.

4. James Gleick, *Chaos: Making a New Science* (New York: Viking, 1987). Gleick's book is credited with popularizing chaos theory. He argues that many events are unpredictable in advance because of their extreme "sensitive dependence on initial conditions."

5. A serious problem for the determinist stance is that, if freedom of behavior is denied, then freedom of thought must also be denied. In the same way that actors' feelings of causing their own behavior must be false, thinkers' feelings of having arrived at thoughts must be false. Without freedom of thought, no thinker can claim to have escaped their own biases in order to arrive at the truth. Their

thoughts and beliefs are just as mechanically conditioned as everything else.

6. Benjamin Libet, *Mind Time: The Temporal Factor in Consciousness*
(Cambridge, MA: Harvard University Press, 2004). In this book Libet summarizes his famous experiments concerning which comes
first: brain processes or subjective choices. His experiments appear
to show that experiences of choice are just "side effects" of brain processes, but this conclusion is much debated.

7. Alfred Mele, *Free: Why Science Hasn't Disproved Free Will* (Oxford:
Oxford University Press, 2014). Mele criticizes epiphenomenal inter-
pretations of the Libet results, claiming to show that the causal force
of mental intentions can survive those and related findings.

8. Marcel Brass, Ariel Furstenberg, and Alfred R. Mele, "Why Neuroscience Does Not Disprove Free Will," *Neuroscience and Biobehavioral
Reviews* 102 (2019): 251–263. In this review article the authors argue
that "brain activation preceding conscious decisions reflects the decision process rather than a decision," and that "conditional intentions
configure the decision process in Libet-type experiments."

9. Kathleen D. Vohs and Jonathan W. Schooler, "The Value of Believing
in Free Will: Encouraging a Belief in Determinism Increases Cheating," *Psychological Science* 19, no. 1 (2008): 49–54, online at University of Minnesota, https://assets.csom.umn.edu/assets/91974.pdf.

10. Roy F. Baumeister, E. J. Masicampo, and Nathan C. DeWall, "Pro-
social Benefits of Feeling Free: Disbelief in Free Will Increases Aggression and Reduces Helpfulness," *Personality and Social Psychology
Bulletin* 35, no. 2 (2009): 260–268.

Chapter 2: The Grand Hierarchy of Human Reality

1. Kennon Sheldon, Cecilia Chen, and Jonathan C. Hilpert, "Understanding Well-Being and Optimal Functioning: Applying the Multi-
level Personality in Context (MPIC) Model," *Psychological Inquiry* 22,
no. 1 (2011): 1–16. This article, along with multiple submitted commentaries and our replies to those commentaries, provides the best
overview of the grand hierarchy approach.

2. Auguste Comte, *Cours de philosophie positive*, vol. 1 (Paris, 1830).

Chapter 3: The Source of Our Free Will

1. Gary Lavergne, *A Sniper in the Tower: The Charles Whitman Murders* (Denton: University of North Texas Press, 1997). This book describes the incidents of that day as well as Whitman's background and history.
2. Mirza Ashraf, "Introduction to the Philosophy of Holism," Thinkers' Forum USA, February 20, 2012, www.thinkersforumusablog.org /archives/216.
3. Harold J. Morowitz, *The Emergence of Everything: How the World Became Complex* (Oxford: Oxford University Press, 2002). Morowitz provides an excellent overview of the concept of emergentism.
4. Robert Melamede, "Dissipative Structures and the Origins of Life," in *Unifying Themes in Complex Systems IV: Proceedings of the Fourth International Conference on Complex Systems,* ed. Ali A. Minai and Yaneer Bar-Yam (Berlin: Springer, 2008), 80–87. Melamede succinctly outlines the connections between dissipative structures and living systems, showing how living things use disorder to create complexity.
5. Bruce Hannon and Matthias Ruth, "Positive and Negative Feedback," in *Dynamic Modeling* (New York: Springer, 2001), 102–110. This article provides a clear overview of both positive and negative feedback as they relate to behavior.
6. George A. Miller, Eugene Galanter, and Karl H. Pribram, *Plans and the Structure of Behavior* (New York: Henry Holt, 1960). This groundbreaking book on the TOTE process is still a classic in the field.

Chapter 4: If We're Free, Why Don't We Feel Free?

1. Edward L. Deci, *Intrinsic Motivation* (New York: Springer, 1975). This book summarizes Deci's early work on this topic.
2. Alfie Kohn, *Punished by Rewards: The Trouble with Gold Stars, Incentive Plans, A's, Praise, and Other Bribes* (Boston: Houghton Mifflin, 1993). Kohn provides a very readable summary of research on how intrinsic motivation can be undermined and its many societal implications.

3. Kendra Cherry, "Drive-Reduction Theory and Human Behavior," Very well Mind, September 17, 2020, www.verywellmind.com/drive-reduction-theory-2795381. This article provides a short introduction to and critique of drive theory.

4. Arlen C. Moller and Kennon M. Sheldon, "Athletic Scholarships Are Negatively Associated with Intrinsic Motivation for Sports, Even Decades Later: Evidence for Long-Term Undermining," *Motivation Science* 6, no. 1 (2019): 43–48.

5. Mark H. White II and Kennon M. Sheldon, "The Contract Year Syndrome in the NBA and MLB: A Classic Undermining Pattern," *Motivation and Emotion* 38, no. 2 (2014): 196–205.

6. Edward L. Deci and Richard M. Ryan, "The Support of Autonomy and the Control of Behavior," *Journal of Personality and Social Psychology* 53, no. 6 (1988): 1024–1037. This was the first article in the literature to emphasize the importance of autonomy support.

7. Kennon M. Sheldon and Anna Watson, "Coach's Autonomy Support Is Especially Important for Varsity Compared to Club and Recreational Athletes," *International Journal of Sports Science and Coaching* 6, no. 1 (2011): 109–123.

8. Kennon M. Sheldon, "Going the Distance on the Pacific Crest Trail: The Vital Role of Identified Motivation," *Motivation Science* 6, no. 2 (2020): 177–181.

9. To complete the picture, the fourth PCT motivation I measured was external motivation—"because I have to," ". . . because my situation is forcing me to," or ". . . because I'll get praise or rewards." This type of motivation was very low in the PCT hikers. It did not change over the summer, and it didn't predict anything, so I haven't talked about it here. But remember, external motivation is often what undermines intrinsic motivation, as in the scholarship athlete study, and as in the contract year study. In the PCT study, external motivation simply wasn't a factor.

10. Kennon M. Sheldon, Tim Kasser, Linda Houser-Marko, Taisha Jones, and Daniel Turban, "Doing One's Duty: Chronological Age, Felt Autonomy, and Subjective Well-Being," *European Journal of Personality* 19, no. 2 (2005): 97–115.

11. Kennon M. Sheldon, Linda Houser-Marko, and Tim Kasser, "Does Autonomy Increase with Age? Comparing the Goal Motivations of College Students and Their Parents," *Journal of Research in Personality* 40, no. 2 (2006): 168–178.

12. Kennon M. Sheldon and Tim Kasser, "Getting Older, Getting Better? Personal Strivings and Psychological Maturity Across the Life Span," *Developmental Psychology* 37, no. 4 (2001): 491–501. In this article we show the age-to-autonomy pattern in yet a third way.

13. Neetu Abad and Kennon Sheldon, "Parental Autonomy Support and Ethnic Culture Identification Among Second-Generation Immigrants," *Journal of Family Psychology* 22, no. 4 (2008): 652–657.

14. Edward L. Deci and Richard Flaste, *Why We Do What We Do: Understanding Self-Motivation* (New York: Putnam: 1996).

15. Lawrence Becker, "Good Lives: Prolegomena," *Social Philosophy and Policy* 9, no. 2 (1992): 15–37.

Chapter 5: Untangling the Mysteries of the Symbolic Self

1. Dan P. McAdams, "Personality, Modernity, and the Storied Self: A Contemporary Framework for Studying Persons," *Psychological Inquiry* 7, no. 4 (1996): 295–321.

2. Constantine Sedikides and John J. Skowronski, "The Symbolic Self in Evolutionary Context," *Personality and Social Psychology Review* 1, no. 1 (1997): 80–102.

3. Some scientists have gone even further, suggesting that all matter is conscious, including nonliving matter. But whether or not this "panpsychism" is true doesn't matter here.

4. Kennon M. Sheldon, Alex Gunz, and Todd R. Schachtman, "What Does It Mean to Be in Touch with Oneself? Testing a Social Character Model of Self-Congruence," *Self and Identity* 11, no. 1 (2012): 51–70.

5. Antonio Damasio, *The Feeling of What Happens: Body and Emotion in the Making of Consciousness* (Fort Worth, TX: Harcourt College, 1999).

6. Thomas Metzinger, *The Ego Tunnel: The Science of the Mind and the Myth of Self* (New York: Basic Books, 2009). This book integrates philosophy and cognitive neuroscience to examine "the myth of the self."

I agree that the self is a myth but also assert that it is important none-theless. It is a "fiction with a function."

7. Jonathan M. Adler, "Living into the Story: Agency and Coherence in a Longitudinal Study of Narrative Identity Development and Mental Health over the Course of Psychotherapy," *Journal of Personality and Social Psychology* 102, no. 2 (2012): 367–389.

Chapter 6: Finding the Symbolic Self in the Brain

1. Randy L. Buckner and Lauren M. DiNicola, "The Brain's Default Network: Updated Anatomy, Physiology and Evolving Insights," *Nature Reviews Neuroscience* 20, no. 10 (2019): 593–608. This article provides a readable recent review of DMN research.

2. Jessica R. Andrews-Hanna, "The Brain's Default Network and Its Adaptive Role in Internal Mentation," *Neuroscientist* 18, no. 3 (2012): 251–270.

3. Randy L. Buckner, Jessica R. Andrews-Hanna, and Daniel L. Schacter, "The Brain's Default Network: Anatomy, Function, and Relevance to Disease," *Annals of the New York Academy of Sciences* 1124 (2008): 1–38.

4. Michael D. Greicius, Guarav Srivastava, Allan L. Reiss, and Vinod Menon, "Default-Mode Network Activity Distinguishes Alzheimer's Disease from Healthy Aging: Evidence from Functional MRI," *Proceedings of the National Academy of Sciences* 101, no. 13 (2004): 4637–4642.

5. Debra A. Gusnard and Marcus E. Raichle, "Searching for a Baseline: Functional Imaging and the Resting Human Brain," *Nature Reviews Neuroscience* 2, no. 10 (2001): 684–694.

6. Frank Van Overwalle, "Social Cognition and the Brain: A Meta-Analysis," *Human Brain Mapping* 30, no. 3 (2009): 829–858.

7. Wanqinq Li, Xiaoqin Mai, and Chao Liu, "The Default Mode Network and Social Understanding of Others: What Do Brain Connectivity Studies Tell Us," *Frontiers in Human Neuroscience* 8, article 74 (2014).

8. Istvan Molnar-Szakacs and Lucina Q. Uddin, "Self-Processing and the Default Mode Network: Interactions with the Mirror Neuron System," *Frontiers in Human Neuroscience* 7, article 571 (2013).

9. George Herbert Mead, *Mind, Self, and Society* (Chicago: University of Chicago Press, 1934). This book explains how human selves are inextricably entwined with the selves of others.

10. Lev Vygotsky, *Mind in Society: The Development of Higher Psychological Processes* (Cambridge, MA: Harvard University Press, 1978). Vygotsky says that external perspectives provide the scaffolding upon which our own internal perspectives are built.

11. Daniel L. Schachter, Donna Rose Addis, and Randy L. Buckner, "Episodic Simulation of Future Events: Concepts, Data, and Applications," *Annals of the New York Academy of Sciences* 1124 (2008).

12. Eric Klinger, *Meaning and Void: Inner Experience and the Incentives in People's Lives* (Minneapolis: University of Minnesota Press, 1977).

13. Buckner et al., "The Brain's Default Network."

14. Jeffrey R. Binder, "Task-Induced Deactivation and the 'Resting' State," *Neuroimage* 62, no. 2 (2012): 1086–1091.

15. Gordon L. Shulman, Julie A. Fiez, Maurizio Corbetta, Randy L. Buckner, Francis M. Miezin, Marcus E. Raichle, and Steven E. Petersen, "Common Blood Flow Changes Across Visual Tasks: II. Decreases in Cerebral Cortex," *Journal of Cognitive Neuroscience* 9, no. 5 (1997): 648–663.

16. Buckner et al., "The Brain's Default Network."

Chapter 7: The Problem of Too *Much* Freedom

1. Suicide is something that other animals just don't do, except in rare and hard-to-interpret cases. For a readable review of this literature, see Richard Pallardy, "Do Animals Commit Suicide?," *Discover*, August 10, 2021, www.discovermagazine.com/planet-earth/do-animals-commit-suicide.

2. Andras Angyal, *Foundations for a Science of Personality* (New York: Viking, 1941). This book foresaw many of the issues that will be considered in this chapter.

3. Daniel Kahneman, *Thinking, Fast and Slow* (New York: Farrar, Straus and Giroux, 2011). Kahneman's book describes automatic thinking (system 1) as the real "hero" of the mind, despite what system 2 may believe about itself. In this book, I ascribe much more agency and importance to system 2, despite its limitations. System 2 is the goal-setter, determining "go" versus "no-go" and monitoring things henceforth.

4. Kennon M. Sheldon, "Becoming Oneself: The Central Role of Self-Concordant Goal Selection," *Personality and Social Psychology Review* 18, no. 4 (2014): 349–365. This article was among the first to apply the concepts of system 1 and system 2 functioning to conscious and nonconscious motivations.

5. Kennon M. Sheldon and Andrew J. Elliot, "Goal Striving, Need Satisfaction, and Longitudinal Well-Being: The Self-Concordance Model," *Journal of Personality and Social Psychology* 76, no. 3 (1999): 482–497. My original thinking on this topic is contained in this article.

6. David C. McClelland, Richard Koestner, and Joel Weinberger, "How Do Self-Attributed and Implicit Motives Differ?," *Psychological Review* 96, no. 4 (1989): 690–702. This article, the first on the topic, was published in psychology's most prestigious journal for integrative new theorizing and is now a classic.

7. Oliver C. Schultheiss and Joyce S. Pang, "Measuring Implicit Motives," in *Handbook of Research Methods in Personality Psychology*, ed. Richard W. Robins, R. Chris Fraley, and Robert F. Krueger (New York: Guilford Press, 2007). In this chapter Schultheiss and Pang summarize how the Picture Story Exercise works.

8. Kennon M. Sheldon and Julia Schüler, "Wanting, Having, and Needing: Integrating Motive Disposition Theory and Self-Determination Theory," *Journal of Personality and Social Psychology* 101, no. 5 (2011): 1106–1123.

9. Kennon Sheldon and Ryan Goffredi, "The Self-Concordance Model: Using Free Will Wisely," in *Oxford Handbook of Self-Determination Theory Research*, ed. Richard Ryan and Edward Deci (forthcoming).

10. Timothy D. Wilson, *Strangers to Ourselves: Discovering the Adaptive Unconscious* (Cambridge, MA: Harvard University Press, 2004).

11. Peter M. Gollwitzer, "Mindset Theory of Action Phases," in *Handbook of Theories of Social Psychology*, vol. 1, ed. Paul A. M. Van Lange, Arie W. Kruglanski, and E. Tory Higgins (Thousand Oaks, CA: Sage, 2012), 526–546. This chapter summarizes the many studies supporting the Rubicon model.

12. Kennon Sheldon, Mike Prentice, and Evgeny N. Osin, "Rightly Crossing the Rubicon: Evaluating Goal Self-Concordance Prior to Selection

Helps People Choose More Intrinsic Goals," *Journal of Research in Personality* 79, no. 3 (2019): 119–129.

Chapter 8: What Brings Happiness

1. Edward Diener, "Subjective Well-Being," *Psychological Bulletin* 95, no. 3 (1984): 542–575. This seminal article has been cited more than twenty thousand times.

2. Sonja Lyubomirsky, Laura King, and Ed Diener published the classic review on this topic, called "The Benefits of Frequent Positive Affect: Does Happiness Lead to Success?" It was published in *Psychological Bulletin* 131, no. 6 (2005): 803–855.

3. Marc Mehu, Anthony C. Little, and Robin I. M. Dunbar, "Duchenne Smiles and the Perception of Generosity and Sociability in Faces," *Journal of Evolutionary Psychology* 5, no. 1 (2007): 183–196.

4. Kennon M. Sheldon, Mike Corcoran, and Melanie Sheldon, "Duchenne Smiles as Honest Signals of Chronic Positive Mood," *Perspectives on Psychological Science* 16, no. 3 (2021): 654–666.

5. John Maynard-Smith and David Harper, *Animal Signals* (Oxford: Oxford University Press, 2003). This book is an evolutionary analysis of the concept of honest signals.

6. Kennon M. Sheldon, Mike Corcoran, and Jason Trent, "The Face of Crime: Apparent Happiness Differentiates Criminal and Non-Criminal Photos," *Journal of Positive Psychology* 16, no. 4 (2020): 551–560.

7. Aristotle's *Nicomachean Ethics* is still widely discussed today, providing a foundational source in the philosophy of ethics and happiness.

8. Frank Martela and Kennon M. Sheldon, "Clarifying the Concept of Well-Being: Psychological Need-Satisfaction as the Common Core Connecting Eudaimonic and Subjective Well-Being," *Review of General Psychology* 23, no. 4 (2019): 458–474. In this article we tried to resolve both lingering and emerging problems in the well-being literature.

9. Although this is unfair to some philosophers, who do incorporate research findings and data into their thinking. For a very basic outline of this field, see "Experimental Philosophy," Wikipedia, https://en.wikipedia.org/wiki/Experimental_philosophy.

10. Dacher Keltner, *Born to Be Good: The Science of a Meaningful Life* (New York: W. W. Norton, 2009). This book provides an excellent review of contemporary emotion research, which paints a rather positive view of basic human nature, absent excessive conflict and trauma.

11. Kennon M. Sheldon, "Integrating Behavioral-Motive and Experiential-Requirement Perspectives on Psychological Needs: A Two Process Perspective," *Psychological Review* 118, no. 4 (2011): 552–569. This article summarizes SDT's basic needs mini-theory from an evolutionary perspective.

12. Harry T. Reis, Kennon M. Sheldon, Shelly L. Gable, Joseph Roscoe, and Richard M. Ryan, "Daily Well-Being: The Role of Autonomy, Competence, and Relatedness," *Personality and Social Psychology Bulletin* 26, no. 4 (2000): 419–435.

13. Kennon M. Sheldon, Andrew J. Elliot, Youngmee Kim, and Tim Kasser, "What's Satisfying About Satisfying Events? Comparing Ten Candidate Psychological Needs," *Journal of Personality and Social Psychology* 80, no. 2 (2001): 325–339. This article remains one of the few studies that has comprehensively tested a large set of candidate psychological needs.

14. Self-esteem was not predicted by SDT, although you can see it as "pride" in this participant's story. Whether self-esteem might also be a basic psychological need remains a complex and controversial topic, and I won't cover it here, beyond saying that Jennifer Crocker and Lora E. Park published an influential article on it in 2003 called "The Costly Pursuit of Self-Esteem," in *Psychological Bulletin* 130, no. 3, pp. 392–414. They summarized the research literature showing the corrosive effects of being overly concerned with one's own self-worth. So, yes, self-esteem feels good, but it may not be worth pursuing as an end in itself.

15. Christopher P. Niemiec, Richard M. Ryan, and Edward L. Deci, "The Path Taken: Consequences of Attaining Intrinsic and Extrinsic Aspirations in Post-College Life," *Journal of Research in Personality* 473, no. 3 (2009): 291–306.

16. Kennon Sheldon, Robert Cummins, and Shanmukh Kamble, "Life Balance and Well-Being: Testing a Novel Conceptual and Measurement Approach," *Journal of Personality* 78, no. 4 (2010): 1093–1134.

17. Kennon M. Sheldon, Alexander Gunz, and Todd R. Schachtman, "What Does It Mean to Be in Touch with Oneself? Testing a Social Character Model of Self-Congruence," *Self and Identity* 11, no. 1 (2012): 51–70.

18. Barbara L. Fredrickson and Thomas Joiner, "Reflections on Positive Emotions and Upward Spirals," *Perspectives on Psychological Science* 13, no. 2 (2018): 194–199.

19. Timothy D. Wilson and Daniel T. Gilbert, "Affective Forecasting," in *Advances in Experimental Social Psychology*, vol. 35, ed. Mark P. Zanna (Amsterdam: Elsevier, 2003), 346–411.

20. Kennon M. Sheldon, Alexander Gunz, Charles P. Nichols, and Yuna Ferguson, "Extrinsic Value Orientation and Affective Forecasting: Overestimating the Rewards, Underestimating the Costs," *Journal of Personality* 78, no. 1 (2010): 149–178.

21. Kennon Sheldon and Mike Corcoran, "Comparing the Current and Long-Term Career Motivations of Artists and Business-People: Is Everyone Intrinsic in the End?," *Motivation and Emotion* 43, no. 5 (2019): 1–14.

22. Carl R. Rogers, "Toward a Modern Approach to Values: The Valuing Process in the Mature Person," *Journal of Abnormal and Social Psychology* 68, no. 2 (1964): 160–167.

23. Kennon M. Sheldon, Jamie Arndt, and Linda Houser-Marko, "In Search of the Organismic Valuing Process: The Human Tendency to Move Towards Beneficial Goal Choices," *Journal of Personality* 71, no. 5 (2003): 835–869.

Chapter 9: The Digital Self

1. Unfortunately our Facebook feeds also reinforce our group identities, often at the expense of other groups; this has the effect of driving groups further apart from each other and fracturing society. In social psychology, this phenomenon was discovered in the early 1960s in pre-internet forms, such as in social groups, and was called *group polarization*. Today, group polarization is happening on a massive scale in the world, and the situation doesn't look good. But that is a topic for a different book.

2. See the Crystal company website at www.crystalknows.com.

3. Alexander Kachur, Evgeny Osin, Denis Davydov, Konstantin Shutilov, and Alexey Novokshonov, "Assessing the Big Five Personality Traits Using Real-Life Static Facial Images," *Scientific Reports* 10, article 8487 (2020).

4. See "Recommendation on the Ethics of Artificial Intelligence," UNESCO, https://en.unesco.org/artificial-intelligence/ethics.

5. Alan M. Turing, "Computing Machinery and Intelligence," *Mind* 59, no. 236 (1950): 433–460.

6. For a description of what it's like to talk with Eugene Goostman, the "fake kid," see Doug Aamoth, "Interview with Eugene Goostman, the Fake Kid Who Passed the Turing Test," *Time*, June 9, 2014, https://time.com/2847900/eugene-goostman-turing-test.

7. John R. Searle, "Minds, Brains, and Programs," *Behavioral and Brain Sciences* 3 (1980): 417–457. Searle argued that a machine that is merely following a set of instructions can never have a mind, understanding, or consciousness.

8. The character Data is played by actor Brent Spiner. There are a number of episodes exploring the issue of his sentience.

9. Alan Watts, *The Wisdom of Insecurity* (New York: Pantheon, 1951). Watts says that our attempts to avoid insecurity and anxiety are crippling to our happiness and development.

10. For a readable short article on this problem, see "The AI Black Box Problem," ThinkAutomation, www.thinkautomation.com/bots-and-ai/the-ai-black-box-problem.

11. For a contemporary discussion of the Ship of Theseus problem and its implications for our feelings of identity, see Maria Popova, "The Ship of Theseus: A Brilliant Ancient Thought Experiment Exploring What Makes You You," *The Marginalian*, www.themarginalian.org/2016/03/08/plutarch-the-ship-of-theseus-ted-ed.

Chapter 10: The Creative Process of Living

1. Much of this research was led by G. Andrew Benjamin. See, for example, G. Andrew H. Benjamin, Alfred W. Kaszniak, Bruce Sales, and Stephen B. Shanfield, "The Role of Legal Education in Producing Psychological Distress Among Law Students and Lawyers," *Law and*

Social Inquiry 11, no. 2 (1986): 225–252. *Law and Social Inquiry* is a journal published on behalf of the American Bar Association.

2. Kennon M. Sheldon and Lawrence S. Krieger, "Does Legal Education Have Undermining Effects on Law Students? Examining Changes in Motivation, Values, and Well-Being," *Behavioral Sciences and the Law* 22, no. 2 (2004): 261–286.

3. Graham Wallas, *The Art of Thought* (Oxford: Oxford University Press, 1926). This book was groundbreaking in many respects.

4. Sébastian Hélie and Ron Sun, "Incubation, Insight, and Creative Problem Solving: A Unified Theory and a Connectionist Model," *Psychological Review* 117, no. 3 (2010): 994–1024.

5. For example, see Lawrence S. Krieger and Kennon M. Sheldon, "What Makes Lawyers Happy? A Data-Driven Prescription to Redefine Professional Success," *George Washington Law Review* 83, no. 2 (2015): 554–627. In this research we found a correlation coefficient between income and SWB of 0.19; for autonomous work motivation and SWB it was 0.55.

6. Andrew T. Jebb, Louis Tay, Ed Diener, and Shigehiro Oishi, "Happiness, Income Satiation and Turning Points Around the World," *Nature Human Behaviour* 2, no. 1 (2018): 33–38. This article examines the point at which income no longer affects SWB. This point differed some across countries but was never higher than $125,000.

7. Kennon M. Sheldon and Lawrence S. Krieger, "Service Job Lawyers Are Happier Than Money Job Lawyers, Despite Their Lower Income," *Journal of Positive Psychology* 9, no. 3 (2014): 219–226.

8. The concept of learned helplessness is one of Martin Seligman's seminal contributions. Seligman and his colleagues showed, first with dogs and then with people, that when animals have no control early on, they prematurely generalize to assume that they'll never have control. Thus they give up even in situations where continued effort would solve the problem. Later research showed that learned helplessness is a powerful explanation for chronic depression.

9. Mihaly Csikszentmihaly, *Flow: The Psychology of Optimal Experience* (New York: Harper and Row, 1990). This book about flow and

flow theory has become a classic in the field. There are important convergences between states of flow and states of intrinsic motivation.

10. Marcia Baxter Magolda, *Authoring Your Life: Developing an Internal Voice to Navigate Life's Challenges* (Sterling, VA: Stylus, 2009).

Epilogue: Living Well Together

1. Thomas Nagel, "What Is It Like to Be a Bat?," *Philosophical Review* 83, no. 4 (1974): 435–450. Nagel argues against reductionism, saying that we must understand consciousness directly in order to understand human behavior—and that this may be impossible.

2. Steven Pinker, *The Better Angels of Our Nature: Why Violence Has Declined* (New York: Penguin, 2011). This book marshaled many kinds of data to argue that human society really is improving, although not as quickly as we might like it to. In his follow-up book, *Enlightenment Now: The Case for Reason, Science, Humanism, and Progress* (New York: Viking, 2018), Pinker argued that seventeenth-century Enlightenment ideals have brought us a long way and that we need to reaffirm our commitment to them.

INDEX

Kennon M. Sheldon is curator's distinguished professor of psychological sciences at the University of Missouri. He is one of the founding researchers of positive psychology, a fellow of the American Psychological Association, and a recipient of the Templeton Foundation Positive Psychology Prize. He lives in Columbia, Missouri.